T0178818

Hospital Logistics and e-Management

Series Editor
Jean-Paul Bourrières

Hospital Logistics and e-Management

Digital Transition and Revolution

Edited by

Philippe Blua
Farouk Yalaoui
Lionel Amodeo
Michaël De Block
David Laplanche

WILEY

First published 2019 in Great Britain and the United States by ISTE Ltd and John Wiley & Sons, Inc.

ISTE Ltd
27-37 St George's Road
London SW19 4EU
UK

www.iste.co.uk

John Wiley & Sons, Inc.
111 River Street
Hoboken, NJ 07030
USA

www.wiley.com

Library of Congress Control Number: 2019944252

British Library Cataloguing-in-Publication Data
A CIP record for this book is available from the British Library
ISBN 978-1-78630-500-8

Contents

Chapter 5. Forecasting Patient Flows into Emergency
Mohamed AFILAL, Lionel AMODEO, Farouk YALAOUI and
Frédéric DUGARDIN

Chapter 6. Positioning and Innovations from the Champagne Sud Hospitals in the World of Hospital Logistics 145
Moïse NOUMBISSI TCHOUPO, Alice YALAOUI, Lionel AMODEO and Farouk YALAOUI

Preface

At a time when new information and communication technology (NICT) is disrupting daily life and seems, day by day, to be exerting greater influence on our private lives, it is informative to study the real impact it may have in the hospital world. We must examine the use to which this may be put in the future. Although health establishments are not best equipped to optimize the use of NICT, there is a favorable shift taking place in mindsets and the use of these technologies.

Approaching these challenges and achieving set objectives are both difficult tasks and cannot be carried out without collaboration between the world of health and the digital world (both industrial and academic). In this book, readers will discover a fruitful collaboration that has existed for several years now between a city hospital, where the number of patients continues to grow, and a research team that is specialized in analyzing data on health and using algorithms for decision making through artificial intelligence.

What impact do these new technologies have on hospitals? Which are the technical solutions that are best suited to the hospital setting? Are health professionals prepared for this digital transformation? Will the quality of healthcare deteriorate?

These are but a few of the questions that leap to the fore today and have received few or no answers yet. While it may be obvious that no sector can escape this transformation, the introduction of technological innovations in the field of health must be studied. This will take place through preventive measures, measures supporting the patient at home and for improving follow-up, both within and outside the hospital.

The objective of this book is to examine how information technology is currently being used in health establishments, to state what should be done and to propose possible uses of NICT, artificial intelligence (AI) and operational research (OR).

This book will give readers the chance to enrich and broaden their knowledge of information systems in hospitals. It illustrates the importance of new technology and how it can transform health. Furthermore, even though every one of us is familiar, in some way, with hospitals (through routine visits or even emergency procedures), the first few chapters offer readers a greater understanding of information systems in hospitals, the data that the hospital uses to function and why optimizing data management and resources may change the quality of healthcare that each patient receives.

The book, thus, provides an overview of the hospital world and lists out the requirements of its health information system. It also studies medical information, its history, supports and challenges. In addition to the challenges and obstacles to the flow of information, we also have logistical flows, which are intimately related to the information flows. Hospital logistics have been broadly explained using the case study of the Champagne Sud hospitals (CSH).

The book presents two studies that emerged from the collaborations between the CSH and university research on how high-performing decision-making tools may draw profiles from these NICT, AI and OR, and use these to improve the quality of service provided to patients and to improve the logistical organization of the hospital.

The first study examines forecasting patient flow into emergency care, and how this could make it possible to improve the management of their admission and the organization of services.

The second study looks at the optimization of the distribution and collection of product flows (food, linen, medicine and materials).

This scientific collaboration is undoubtedly ushering in the hospital of the future, and presages important and essential advances.

The final chapters discuss in detail the studies and flagship solutions that have been proposed in this collaboration. After many years, and after a nervous beginning, marked by the declaration that, "it is never possible to predict how many patients will come into emergency care", we have been able to help the hospital in Troyes predict patient inflow with an accuracy rate of almost 95%.

This project may be summarized by a simple motto: using data, it is always possible to predict or foresee the future in a way that benefits everyone.

Farouk YALAOUI
July 2019

Hospitals and Management

1.1. Introduction

At a time when new information and communication technologies (NICTs) are disrupting our daily life and, every day, exerting greater influence on our private life, it is instructive to study what impact they will have in the hospital field. It is important to ask ourselves how these technologies can be used in the future. Let us state this right away: health establishments are not best prepared to optimally use NICT. Information technology (IT) has been disliked in this field for quite some time.

The hospital world is one of those rare spheres where, even today, secretaries frequently use typewriters for letters. The blame for this can be apportioned among several parties: any number of health ministers have extended an outdated system, preferring written documents and physical consultations over paper-free exchanges; any number of hospital directors have regarded digitization as an expense rather than an investment; any number of doctors have resisted attempts to digitize medical files.

The aim of this chapter is not to point fingers, but to establish the current state of IT in health establishments, specify what needs to be done and to look at the possible uses that can be made of NICT.

Chapter written by Philippe BLUA.

1.2. Imperfections in hospital information technology

Hospital IT systems often suffer from the same shortcomings – from seven deadly sins! These are as follows: the engineer's dream, the lack of support, the jargon, hospital-centrism, ergonomic heresy, forgetting productivity and the absence of an IT strategy.

Here again, I do not wish to accuse any specific entity, especially not the IT teams, who are doing their best in a hostile world. The weight of local tradition, budget problems, the present offering available, generational problems, power structures within an institution as complex as a hospital – all these are so many obstacles to finding the *optimal* solution.

One can be aware of these difficulties and still be clear-sighted and wish to do better – so let us first begin with a diagnosis of the problems that often plague hospital IT systems. The engineer's dream is characterized by a constant striving for technological excellence at the cost of all other considerations, especially those of cost, utility and functionality. In all my postings as directors, I have always had the privilege of having an office telephone with at least 30 buttons on it (I have had machines with up to 60 buttons!) and – I assume – countless functions that they can perform. I say "I assume" because I was almost never told how exactly this telephone worked. On the few occasions it *was* explained to me, I remembered nothing, either because most of the functions were of no use to me or because I used them so rarely that I forgot how they worked (often a complex process) in the interim. I only ever used about 10 or 20%, at most, of the functions offered by these technological marvels – the perfect example of sheer waste born out of the best of intentions. The people who had bought it wished to offer me the ideal product, without considering the cost, what I would really require from a telephone, nor the ergonomics of the apparatus; sometimes I was not even told about the functions or working, because it seemed so obvious to the technician! What was true for the telephone holds true for pure IT: nobody has seen it fit to explain to me the in-house programs on my PC desktop and I have never bothered about them since I never use them.

The lack of support is another recurrent failing. Without an adequate budget, future users of these programs never receive sufficient training. The effectiveness of the training is very rarely verified after a few weeks or months of use. Newcomers who may have missed the initial training are sometimes trained on the job. Being chiefly passed on through oral instruction, the available knowledge on equipment and software soon peters away and consequently we also lose out on the professional benefits that could have resulted from it. It is essential to remember that oral transmission of learning is not the best tool to safeguard and record information. Furthermore, even the simplest software needs to be learned, especially since knowing how to run it is not the same as being able to use it correctly. One simply needs to sit through a few Powerpoint presentations to see the truth of this. Who has not seen an overcrowded slide, with the font size so small that even those right in front of the screen are unable to read what is written? If the text is legible, then the presenter insists on reading it out verbatim to their literate audience. Thus, this presentation tool, intended to make material come alive and be easily memorized, becomes an instrument of torture and boredom and, therefore, leads to poor attention and forgetfulness.

The communication gaps between the computer scientists and the rest of the hospital staff contribute to this. Of course, every profession has its own jargon and guards it jealously, but I find that the chasm between the IT world and the medical world is especially wide, despite the medical world seeing a wave of newcomers who take the Internet and digital resources as much for granted as their seniors do running water and electricity.

Hospital-centrism is another problem that is not only restricted to the context of IT. We are only too prone to reproduce what already exists in health establishments, without looking to other domains for innovations. Thus, we keep looking out for references to hospitals in the range of functions offered by products or services that are really not specialized. I have seen this with elevators. What difference can there be in how people are transported up and down a building, regardless of whether they are sick, healthy, nurses or bankers? The only result this has is discouraging many companies and reducing the number of suppliers to a hospital.

These suppliers often tend to perpetuate this herd mentality by offering one hospital what is already being used in other hospitals. They can thus avoid renewing their service offerings. For instance, I have had architects suggest, for a new building under construction, light fittings that are identical to those in another hospital building that was built a dozen years ago, as if technology and design have not changed in over a decade! This also exists in the IT world. To give you just one example out of many, medical file editors still function with an MS Office suite type of ergonomics, light years removed from the Android and iOS models that dominate the world today. All of this limits innovation and ends up costing the hospital dearly.

The lack of ergonomics is common and is almost a trademark of first-generation mass-market IT products, especially in their PC versions. As proof I offer this anecdotal, but illuminating, question: why did it take until Windows 10 before users no longer had to click on "Start" to shut down their PC? One of the reasons for this situation being as it is that designers of IT tools sometimes forget to step into the shoes of future users or even end up giving greater value to their comfort compared to that of the users. For example, on Windows PC keyboards you need to press on two buttons for a colon (:) but only one for a semicolon (;). But who really uses a semicolon? The average end-user, who chiefly uses the colon for punctuation, very rarely uses the semicolon and it is in fact the programmer who needs to use it very frequently. However, programmers make up a tiny fraction of the overall users of a PC! End-users of technological products are looking for practical and, if possible, aesthetically-pleasing products; as with any other consumer, they prefer products with a good design. It was based on this observation that Steve Jobs relaunched Apple – and so successfully that the company eventually overtook Windows to reach the number one spot on the stock markets. It began with the iMac in 1998, which was infinitely more elegant than the PCs of that era; then came the iPod, which wiped out the Walkman; and then, finally, the smartphone that dethroned Nokia and Blackberry.

Of course, hospital staff are subject to the purchasing decisions carried out by their institution. But though they lack the power to choose the product that pleases them, they can still ignore that which is offered to them. Passive resistance results in an enormous loss of money, efficiency and energy, even if it is overcome – which is not always the case. Then again, IT is an investment. At a time when hospital budgets are being strictly controlled, they must improve productivity. Unfortunately, this imperative need is sometimes forgotten. It may even happen that the IT products used add to a person's workload instead of reducing it. Lawmakers have sometimes contributed to this by mandating, for many long years, that hospitals conserve paper records, as well as digitized records. While this requirement has been lifted, it has not completely solved the problem: even today, physical medical files often co-exist with the digitized files.

More generally, investment in IT is only rarely accompanied by the implementation of a programme that studies and produces figures for the return on investment. One of the reasons for this gap is that IT has almost never been at the heart of hospital strategy. As Seneca said, "If one does not know to which port one is headed, no wind is favorable." In this respect, the law that made it compulsory for hospitals within one territory to work together was immensely innovative as it resulted in the intercommunication of information systems becoming a priority. However, in doing this, it also highlighted a sad reality: the French hospital system, whether public or private, is not exactly at the vanguard of the digital revolution. In certain fields, in fact, it trails far behind. Medical secretaries are, perhaps, the last members of the secretarial world who still spend a large amount of their time typing up letters. Slim consolation: this is not unique to any one country. According to a recent study, the field of health is one of the four sectors of activity, worldwide, that are the least permeable to NICT. This situation is not tenable in the long run. The question of how to effectively use NICT must be central to all considerations related to the hospital.

1.3. Essentials for high-quality IT systems in hospitals

This system must, at the very least, be the focus of strategic reflection, add value, be open and flexible and adapt itself to the needs of users, and be receptive to what is being done in other sectors of activity. The first essential requirement is that digitization be integrated into hospital strategy. It must be used to implement the hospital plan.

This requires being able to distinguish between the essential and the ancillary. If the objective is to improve cooperation between two establishments, then both must try adopting the same (or at least compatible), software, even if they do not offer all the desired functionalities.

This implies being able to differentiate between the tool and the objective. Digitizing a surgical unit is not the end – simply the means. The final objective of this may be to optimize the use of time slots. This, ultimately, requires that not too many projects are started at the same time and in parallel, as there is the risk of being unable to finish any of them or of having delays pile up.

The second obligation is that the investment in IT must be productive. It must result in added value, i.e. it must either bring in greater financial gains or bring in an additional service to users and staff. The financial gain may consist of a reduction in costs or an increase in profits by offering a new service that attracts new users. This always happens by striving for an economic optimum, which may not necessarily be technologically ideal. Indeed, the optimal product is not necessarily the most successful or the most sophisticated. It is the product that offers the greatest advantages in terms of gains in productivity, acceptance by users, ease of management and use, durability, adaptability, price (acquisition as well as maintenance) and technical qualities. In order to realize these gains, we must, of course, carry out any reorganizing that the new IT tool may bring about. Thus, we must study the impact that the new tool has on work and manage any changes brought about beyond the initial training. What tasks can be removed? What modifications can be introduced to how work is organized? How can you improve the tracking of activity?

The durability of the product is a crucial question. Beware of "in-house" software that no one is able to modify, or even maintain, once the developer has left the building. This may seem obvious and this practice was already being criticized in the 1990s. However, it survives even today in some establishments. Beware of fringe suppliers. While one may bet on a start-up, it is a different and far riskier matter altogether to take a chance on an organization that has never succeeded in capturing a significant share of the market. Newcomers must also be given training, otherwise there is the risk that the equipment will be used less and less often.

Above all, we must ensure that the product is flexible. In the age of the digital revolution and at a time when all hospitals in an administrative region are being brought together, IT systems in hospitals must be adaptable and open. This is because new practices and new expectations are constantly arising, and there is an ever-growing need to communicate with other actors in the region. Another requirement: adapting to users. Digitization itself does not guarantee simplification, savings in time or greater safety. Those designing the tool must put themselves in the shoes of future users and pay close attention to details in their daily functioning. There is no sense in increasing the number of functionalities if they are not practically useful. The more complex a software is to use, the more time is spent on training and the lower the gains in productivity. Furthermore, it brings the risk of error or dysfunction.

A tool has greater acceptance when it is useful in daily life and will become familiar. Ergonomics is something that IT systems often forget about. This causes an enormous financial loss in the form of lost time. When it comes to learning a new tool, the less user-friendly a product is, the longer and more expensive is the training. In the introduction phase, *learning by doing* is tiresome and causes discontent. When the time comes to use the software, there will be time lost in handling it and, a more serious problem, shortcuts will be taken. One of the reasons paper files on patients still exist is because of how user-unfriendly most digitized medical files are.

The final requirement is to pay attention to what is happening in other places. Benchmarking allows us to verify that our processes are not outdated and allows us to save time by avoiding reinventing solutions that already exist, while obtaining the best prices by accessing mass-market products.

This technological awakening cannot be restricted to the world of French hospitals, but must encompass other sectors of activities and other countries. Doing things differently is always possible and can offer real opportunities – it becomes an obligation in the digital revolution.

1.4. Hospital IT systems of the future

From 2002 onwards, humanity entered a new era: the digital age. This is characterized not only by an unprecedented accumulation of data (Figure 1.1) but also by the massive exchange of these data (Figure 1.2).

This computer/Internet coupling is changing the world by ushering in the largest democratization of knowledge since Gutenberg, and by changing lifestyles, creating new sectors of economic activity, and overturning existing equilibria and hierarchies. And all this is taking place at a speed never before been seen in human history. It took two centuries for writing to pass from Mesopotamia to Egypt and 80 years for the printing press to travel beyond Europe. But all it took was 20 years, less than one generation, for the Internet to become a global phenomenon. In 1992, there were 26 websites and in 2014 this number reached 1 billion. There were 16 million Internet users in 1995, and over 3 billion in 2015. Today, there are only two regions in the world where less than half the population has internet access: the African continent and the Indian subcontinent. No sector of activity can remain sheltered from this tsunami for very long. Even if the hospital world (and not only in France) remains one of the most refractory, the future of hospital IT systems will be constructed around NICT. This implies gambling on mobility, revisiting patient–hospital relations, opening up hospital networks to other actors in the sphere of health, reflecting on the use of data and overseeing the development of robotization. Hospital IT systems are still largely static and designed for PCs. This is a completely outdated approach at a time when the number of mobile users has exceeded that of computer-based Internet users in 2014, when smartphones and tablets represent 90% of devices that give people access to the Internet and when the remainder chiefly consists of laptops. The hospital of the future is not 2.0, it is 4G.

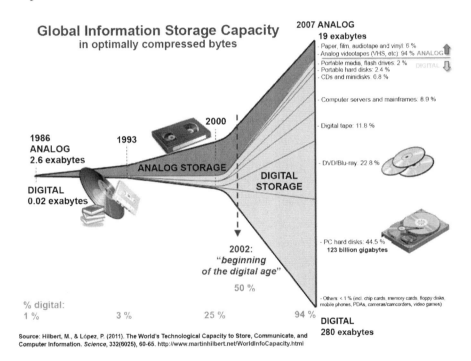

Global Information Storage Capacity
in optimally compressed bytes

2007 ANALOG
19 exabytes
- Paper, film, audiotape and vinyl: 6 %
- Analog videotapes (VHS, etc): 94 %   ANALOG
- Portable media, flash drives: 2 %   DIGITAL
- Portable hard disks: 2.4 %
- CDs and minidisks: 6.8 %

- Computer servers and mainframes: 8.9 %

- Digital tape: 11.8 %

- DVD/Blu-ray: 22.8 %

- PC hard disks: 44.5 %
  123 billion gigabytes

- Others: < 1 % (incl. chip cards, memory cards, floppy disks, mobile phones, PDAs, cameras/camcorders, video games)

DIGITAL
280 exabytes

2000

1986
ANALOG
2.6 exabytes

1993

ANALOG STORAGE

DIGITAL
STORAGE

DIGITAL
0.02 exabytes

2002:
"beginning
of the digital age"

50 %

% digital:
1 %   3 %   25 %   94 %

Source: Hilbert, M., & López, P. (2011). The World's Technological Capacity to Store, Communicate, and Computer Information. *Science*, 332(6025), 60-65. http://www.martinhilbert.net/WorldInfoCapacity.html

Figure 1.1. *Global storage capacity (Hilbert and Lôpez 2011)*

This implies changing models in terms of equipment, but also changing computer programmes, which can no longer be designed with the Microsoft-type ergonomics, but must follow the iOS/Android model that the large majority are familiar with. This will reduce the time spent by staff in learning the programmes and will make it possible to move toward the patient, as the Internet will revolutionize hospital–patient relations. It is already doing this outside the hospital, almost working against hospitals! This is the impact of sites such as Doctissimo, or WebMD where the patient can directly look up their symptoms and treatment or look for second opinions. These include comments on social networks. It is time that health establishments address this and establish a relationship that inspires confidence in patients by handing back power to them and getting them to work on their own health. The Internet offers the means to share a medical case-file in real time. The patient can carry out the admission formalities from home. A chronic patient can use connected devices for remote monitoring of their parameters and any changes in their condition. It offers a means to transmit information, medical advice and to remind the patient about the modalities of a treatment. And all this occurs at lowered costs and potentially enormous gains in productivity!

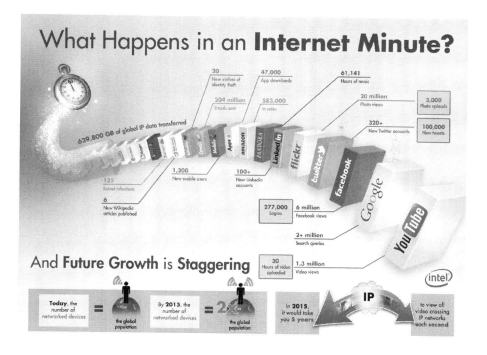

Figure 1.2. *What happens in one Internet Minute?*
(Long 2013)

The cost aspect must be emphasized. For a long time, hospitals have worked with specialized industrial establishments that only conceived of transmitting medical information using extremely costly models. Today, the NICT industry offers connected objects and encrypted information transmission tools at ridiculously low costs and with astounding performances. The hour of low-cost medicine-at-a-distance is here, bringing with it the ability to share information with other health professionals. In the medical set-up of tomorrow, the patient will be able to fill in their own medical file. Consequently, this file can be shared at once among those health professionals, who are responsible for following up on the patient in the city and/or with the medico-social institute where they may be admitted. The medical file of the future will no longer be a hospital file. It will become a shared folder that other actors have the right to consult and edit, based on rules and regulations that must be established. In order to be efficient, these files will integrate more and more medico-social data, or even information on the patient's lifestyle (sports they play, diet, etc.). It is crucial for hospitals to participate in, or even initiate, this process so that they are able to control it and the data that are thus created. The use of these data is a key issue. If digitized, all the books in the Grand Library at Alexandria would have fit onto a 1 terabyte (TB) disk. In 1986, there was 2.6 million TB of data in the world (Figure 1.1). In 2012, this number had been multiplied by a billion. Every day in 2017 saw 2.6 million TB of data being added – as much as existed overall in 1986. The hospital has its part to play in this process. We have entered the era of Big Data.

Today, less than one-third of French companies are questioned about their use of their data. This number is probably even smaller for health establishments. This is a mistake because, if used well, this information may allow health establishments to better analyze their activity, get to know their patients better, contribute to medical research and enhance their performance by practicing predictive analysis. As concerns daily functioning, the use of data will make it possible to process and correlate more information, have access to information in real time, couple information and geolocalization. This is in order to facilitate a better understanding of events and, therefore, to facilitate decision making, and to develop decision-making aids via access to appropriate instructions or similar examples.

With respect to patient awareness, the use of their medical file and the information that they can supply themselves (tracking their parameters, diet, activity, etc.) may generate alerts on changes in their state of health. Where medical research is concerned, it is possible to imagine storing an unlimited amount of data for an equally unlimited duration, to make it easier to access these data, to facilitate grouping within these data using algorithms and, by doing so, to confirm or invalidate working hypotheses. As concerns the predictive aspect, collaborative work between the University of Technology of Troyes and the Troyes hospital center has shown that it is possible to anticipate Emergency (ER) activities and the availability of beds with a percentage of error smaller than 10% using the data on activity from earlier years.

The final topic to consider is the use of robots. These robots already exist in hospitals, but often in archaic forms – unwieldy and with little autonomy, thus, for logistical transport or the distribution of medication. However, a new market – still shaky, but promising – is opening up. This is based on low-cost robots that are more autonomous and capable of interacting with patients. There now exist courier robots that cost less than 10,000 euros (about 11,000 USD). This is a sector that must be closely followed. However, it is also important to keep in mind that the interactions with patients are not carried out through the robot as much as through the screen they carry, and thus, it is important to focus on the applications present on this screen.

1.5. Conclusion

To conclude, we must focus on the glaring need to place NICT at the heart of new missions for health establishments. The hospital as an institution is lagging in this field. This is a danger but also an opportunity – appropriate benchmarking of other sectors of activity will allow us to advance faster by replicating good ideas and avoiding reproducing the errors. We also need to set up ethics committees to look into this because Big Data can easily morph into Big Brother. In 'Nineteen Eighty Four', George Orwell imagined a totalitarian world where each individual was spied on by a screen that was always on in their home. Today, we willingly and happily buy a smartphone that is constantly tracking us and, every day, learns a little more about us so that it can offer us even more customized services. These services will soon include improved health – but where is the line between helping and intruding on privacy?

1.6. References

Doctissimo [Online]. Available at: http://www.doctissimo.fr [Accessed 22 December 2018].

Hilbert, M., Lôpez, P. (2011). The World's Technological Capacity to Store, Communicate, Compute Information. *Science*, 332(6025), 60–65.

Long, L. (2013). *What Happens in an Internet Minute* [Online]. Available at: http://www.dailyinfographic.com/what-happens-in-an-internet-minute-infographic [Accessed 4 December 2018].

Orwell, G. (1972). *1984*. Folio, Paris.

Sénèque. *Le Figaro : citations* [Online]. Available at: http://evene.lefigaro.fr/citations/seneque [Accessed 3 January 2019].

The Hospital and its IT System: Where it is Right Now and What it Needs

2.1. Introduction

To gain a good understanding of the challenges related to digitization and computerization, that is, IT systems in hospitals, it is important to review the history of how IT has been used in hospitals in order to more clearly envisage its future.

How far back, exactly, did computerization begin in hospitals? We find reports from the early 1970s of pilot studies of computerization in hospitals, first in the United States and then in Europe (for instance, in Sweden and Switzerland). In this period, an industrial offering of computerized services for hospitals was gradually developed with:

– companies that specialized in health informatics (HBO, SAIC Care, SMS, Technicon);

– hardware manufacturers such as HP or IBM that wished to diversify their offerings.

For a long time, France was absent from the HMS (Hospital Management Software) market for reasons that were both financial (inadequate budgets) as well as strategic (it relied on consortia of hospitals). There emerged several

Chapter written by Michaël DE BLOCK.

regional hospital informatics centers (RHIC), some of which have since disappeared.

For readers who would like more information on this period, we point them to (Degoulet *et al.* 2003). Computerization in French hospitals in the 1980s and 1990s took place chiefly at the administrative level. It focused on economic and financial management, payments, billings and patient stays, with, the emergence of IT streams that are still used today (CPAGE, Pastel, etc.) as well as "in-house" software that were difficult to maintain or interface.

This period saw the creation of the first hospital informatics systems and featured analysts, programmers, developers and desk operators. At this time, the post of "Head of Hospital Informatics" was not seen as a necessary one. At the legislative level in France, the first text that spoke of informatics in the hospital world came out in 1982 and spoke of the "program to medicalize information systems" (PMIS) ("programme de médicalisation des systèmes d'information" (PMSI)). This was the first clearly stated vision of using an information system to evaluate hospital activity.

However, it was not until the official circular no. 275, dated January 6, 1989, that the French Ministry of Health officially recognized the concept of a hospital information system (HIS). Circular no. 275 defined HIS in an establishment as "everything related to information, the rules governing how it is circulated and processed for daily use, the modes of management and evaluation as well as its strategic decision-making process". In 2000, Gérard Ponçon provided a more comprehensive definition of HIS in his book *Le management du système d'information hospitalier : La fin de la dictature technologique* ("The management of hospital information systems: The end of technological dictatorship") (Ponçon 2000): "The hospital information system is inserted into the constantly evolving organization, the 'hospital'. This system, based on predetermined rules and operating protocols, can acquire data, evaluate and process the date using information technology or organizational tools, distribute information containing a high added value to all internal or external partners of the establishment, collaborating on a common project that works towards a specific goal – namely that of managing a patient and their recovery". However, the earliest electronic patient records (EPR) that interfaced with hospital administrative processes (HAP) only trickled out around the early 2000s, comprising chiefly of IMS (identities/movement/stays) bureaucratic functions and NGAP ratings. This gradually led to information bouncing around between the paper files and the digitized records, without any true added value and, thus, led to a highly contested view of hospital informatics.

A new chapter was ushered in through changes in the ways hospital were financed in France. Until 2003, health establishments were financed in several different ways depending on their legal status (financing of establishments). From 2003 onward, a system based on a price-per-task became the only legal means of financing medicine, surgery and obstetric (MSO) activities in both public and private establishments. This system was based on a common classification of medical actions (CCMA), which was gradually implemented from 2004 onward ("codifying" and then "pricing"). It was, thus, decided that one part of the residual annual financing would be continued, complemented by the value of activity data from the PMIS. This valuation of activity increased every year: 10% in 2004, 25% in 2005, 35% in 2006, 50% in 2007 and 100% in 2008.

This method of working gradually led to hospital directors and the medical team growing more interested in EPRs (CCMA input screen). The "contrat de bon usage du médicament" (contract for the proper use of medication) (CBUM – Decree no. 2005–1023 dated August 24, 2005) heightened this interest, leading to an enforced computerization of the medical prescription market. Doctors were forced to start using IT tools. Practices changed and the planning of computerized services slowly became the guiding principle for care services. Indeed, certain medicotechnical specializations (radiology, laboratories, nuclear medicine, coronary angiogram, etc.) surged ahead of other fields as they increasingly used digitized files as a task management tool. We speak here of the computerization of the workflow, starting from the time the patient arrives at the reception desk to the generation of the test reports. In the absence of clear directives, and especially given the lack of adequately developed general EPRs, HIS slowly became a patchwork of different specialist software.

Under these conditions, users grew more dissatisfied with the duplication of patient files (which were maintained in both paper and computerized form) and the need to keep recopying data. IT departments were faced with the need to put in place interfaces between the different software and also with the biomedical ecosystem (picture archiving and communication system (PACS), monitors, automatons, etc.).

Toward 2010, HIS played a more prominent role in the hospital, but it began to seem like a liability, a needless expense and, above all, a risky domain whose malfunctions disrupted the balance within the hospitals. To illustrate how these information systems evolved within hospitals, let us examine the case of the Troyes hospital center. The IT department of the Troyes hospital was established in 1985. It initially consisted of a "large computer system" that depended on the RHIC at Reims for 15 years. At the time, some tens of computers and a few "in-house" developments made up the IT center in a hospital. Toward the end the 1990s, the Troyes hospital decided to exit the Reims RHIC.

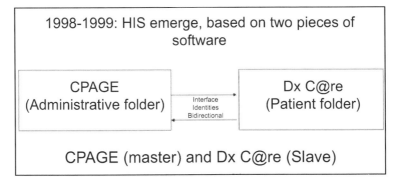

Figure 2.1. *The birth of the HIS*

Ten years later, in 2008, the HIS had become a liability, a field that represented large expenses and a source of risks for the hospital, which decided to organize an external audit. With 70 "specialized" software and hundreds of interfaces, the Troyes HIS had become impossible to maintain.

Toward the late 2000s, the fragility of the HIS led the hospitals to consider a new step they called, "the urbanization of the information system", a process that made it possible to comprehensively describe the information system and provide a well-reasoned arrangement of the "specialization-specific" layers that was functional, applicative and technologically sound. In 2006, the group for the modernization of hospital information systems (GMHIS) published a study on HIS urbanization and, in France, this study became the reference text for HIS urbanization. Today, it is the ANAP (the national agency for support for the performance of health and medicosocial establishments) that manages these aspects (see *Architecture et urbanisation des systèmes* (The Architecture and Urbanization of Systems)) by the Groupement pour la modernisation du système d'information hospitalier (Group for the modernization of the hospital information system). Hospitals gradually integrated the broad suggestions from this study to reinforce their HIS and today these modifications are a prerequisite in any digital hospital (DH) program: organizing competencies, virtualization, clustering, backup, system and interface surveillance (EAI), identity monitoring and unique reference for structure, identities/movement/stays (IMS), and the security of information systems. The progressive upgrading of HIS not only rationalized, stabilized and sustained them, but also led to a progressive transformation of the field of hospital informatics: the IT department became the Directorate of Information Services (with the appearance of the post of Head of the Hospital Informatics Project) and is today the Directorate of Digital Information (DDI), which is ready to take up the challenge of establishing a territorial digital network. The HIS became the instrument for sharing virtual information and supporting patient care within the hospital and also outside the hospital (putting in place health networks, portals and secure messaging systems), which has become even more significant with the implementation of the regional healthcare consortia (or *Groupes hospitaliers de territoire,* GHT) from July 1, 2016. It links technical and functional know-how with communication in a society where networks now play a decisive role, while within the field of health more and more medical deserts arise and financial resources are shrinking.

Hospital informatics thus started out as a simple support, went on to become a management and billing tool and today represents a driving force for cooperation and quality in the field of health. Any hospital that does not invest adequately in this field is likely to face significant repercussions in the future.

This is what we will illustrate now, basing ourselves on eight core areas of cooperation and quality that are associated with an efficient digital ecosystem for hospitals.

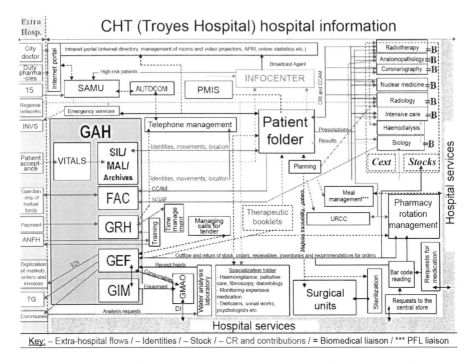

Figure 2.2. *The Troyes hospital information system. For a color version of this figure, see www.iste.co.uk/blua/hospital.zip*

2.2. Cooperation and quality

2.2.1. *Area 1*

For about a decade now, public authorities have launched a variety of projects to help hospitals optimize their information systems (hospital schemes in 2007 and 2012). Subsidies were given without verifying the implementation of the projects and, unfortunately, this money was often used for sectors other than that of optimizing the HIS. Some Directorate of Information Systems (DIS) even spoke about "hospital hodgepodges", making it impossible to carry out any real urbanization project. Conscious of this situation, the Care Services Directorate (CSD) brought in some changes regarding how the subsidies would work: the hospital digitization program (2013–2017) was much more draconian than its predecessor. First of all, it specified some basic prerequisites (ISP, DRP, risk analyses, etc.) in order to apply for the subsidy and also specified objectives that had to be achieved (the digitization of targeted communications, prescriptions, the process for making appointments, etc.). Note that 30% of the amount would be paid at the start of the project and the rest would be paid when the objectives were achieved. If they were not achieved by the end of the program (2017), the hospital would be obliged to reimburse the initial 30% that they received. The sums that were received for modernizing the HIS were substantial, but the formalism and work needed to put in place the prerequisites, as well as to achieve the goals, required competencies that hospital IT teams had to acquire – now more than ever before, they had to state what they were going to do, carry out what they promised and prove to the authorities that this had been well implemented in order to obtain the funding that was essential for the maintenance and evolution of an IT system that had now become vital to the hospital. This first area of work highlights the need to have competent teams and, in particular, HIS project managers who have been trained on courses, receiving for example a Diploma in Hospital IT Systems and Logistics, which would provide them with the foundation needed to carry out onerous and time-consuming administrative formalities that are, nonetheless, essential for the smooth functioning of the HIS.

2.2.2. *Area 2*

The French Health Authority (Haute Autorité de Santé (HAS)) is an independent public authority that plays a role in regulating the health system through quality control. It carries out its tasks in fields such as the evaluation of health products, professional practices and the organization of care and public health. The HAS certifies health establishments and accredits practitioners in some disciplines in order to evaluate and improve the quality of care and patient safety in healthcare facilities and in community medicine since 2010, and especially since late-2013, HIS have become an important criterion for certification. In a very positive move, the HAS decided to combine the DH program with the certification of healthcare facilities based on a proposal from the Directorate for Care Organization (DCO). Since the September 2013 inspections:

– the 5(a) (information system) criteria and the 5(b) (the security of information systems) criteria have been systematically examined;

– all the DH indicators associated with manual criteria became useful and complementary tools for appraising different components.

A working knowledge of these criteria is, therefore, indispensable, regardless of the actual state of development of one's HIS. Areas 1 and 2 are closely linked and investing in one (for financial reasons) makes it possible to respond to the needs of the next one (in order to certify one's institution). Directors of institutions are growing increasingly conscious of this and if they are unable to recruit or train competent IT staff, they turn to the regional e-health healthcare cooperation consortium (HCC) for support in this enterprise of formalizing the necessary documents.

2.2.3. *Area 3*

For some years now, new certifications at national and international levels have made it possible to enhance the image of a hospital and, thus, make the work carried out by the IT team more important in the eyes of the board of directors and trustees. Two examples that are particularly striking at present are:

– Healthcare Information Management Systems Society (HIMSS): a not-for-profit organization dedicated to the optimal use of information technology and management systems to improve health. Its mission is to transform the health sector through the efficient use of ICT. HIMSS designs and initiates health practices as well as public policies through their expertise on content, professional development, research and media tools in order to improve the quality, security and access to healthcare, while curbing costs. At present, about 10 healthcare institutions in France have been able to obtain a "level 6" certification (out of a total of seven levels). HIMMS is really "the place to be" in this sector, with the recent creation of a French unit (HIMSS French Community) for European francophone communities (France, Belgium, Luxembourg and Switzerland);

– when designing the specifications and choices in software, hospital IT engineers must now consider prescription assistance programs (PAP) or drug dispensing assistance programs (DAP). The law on reinforcing the safety of drugs and health products, which came into effect on December 29, 2011, made it compulsory to certify software for prescription assistance (PAPs) and software for help in dispensing drugs (DAPs) in pharmacies from April 1, 2016. The French Health Authority supervises this task (Haute autorité de Santé 2017).

2.2.4. *Area 4*

As we discussed earlier, hospitals, and thus HIS, revolve around financial considerations. Two current requirements can mobilize hospital IT personnel in the short and medium term. These projects would be impossible to carry out without a high-performing HIS and good methodology. Not respecting these requirements may have disastrous financial consequences for the health institution:

– the Helios version 2 standard exchange protocol (SEP V2) is the solution for virtualizing invoices, payment orders and pay slips. In use from 2008 onward, it was mandated that from April 1, 2016 the PES V2 would replace the various "flat" transmission protocols for invoices and pay orders, which had to be duplicated with a paper communication when sending it to the treasury (and, following this, Chorus Portail Pro on January 1, 2017) (for more on this, please refer to the text on standard exchange protocol);

– the individual invoicing of health institutions (IIHE) or FIDES (Facturation Individuelle des établissements de santé – individual billing of health facilities): Article 63 of the Financing Law marked the end of the practice of generalizing individual invoicing from March 1, 2016 for all public and private, not-for-profit health institutions carrying out MSO activities (procedures and out-patient consultations, initially). By this deadline (March 1, 2016), a large part of invoices related to activity in health institutions would rely on similar processes to generate high-quality invoices. Adapting the organization, training and professionalization of teams, and the increased reliability of data are all building blocks that must be put in place without delay (for more on this, we can consult the FIDES project report made in parliament (Ministère de la Santé 2017).

2.2.5. *Area 5*

The financial environment is becoming harder. With a reduction in the ONDAM (National objective of health insurance expenditure) (Wikipedia 2017), hospitals must find a way to increase their takings in order to balance budgets. PMIS thus becomes even more important in the organization of the hospital. This subject will be discussed in more detail in Chapter 4.

IT tools, and especially putting in place a Medical Informatics Department (MID) info-center, along with applications such as the PMIS pilot or

AMEDIM, make it possible to move ahead in this direction hospitals must also be able to leverage alternative sources of income, such as:

– a functional unit for floating medicine in care homes for the elderly;

– a kangaroo mother care unit in neonatology;

– trackers to identify malnourished patients in order to increase the number of consultations with dieticians.

In each case, the Health Informatics Project Head will be required to modify the parameters of the HIS to help health professionals in understanding and grasping new organizations that will allow them to add new paid services, and they may even need to help the MID in managing a regional PMIS in the context of a regional healthcare consortium.

2.2.6. *Axe 6*

The battle against the creation of medical deserts is not simply a metaphor; it is a reality that isolates villages, condemns small hospitals and overturns rural life. Initiatives are being intensified throughout France to battle against these deserts by using information technology and communication. Among many encouraging experiments that have been carried out, there are several telemedicine projects, including:

– the implementation of the TeleAVC (AVC is the French medical term for "stroke") which establishes a telemedicine link between a conventional hospital and a teaching hospital in Reims to improve the chances of recovery for a patient who suffers a stroke in a rural health center;

– the implementation of the remote interpretation of radiology reports between a small hospital and a larger hospital center to prevent the shutting down of the radiology department in the smaller institution and to also prevent the local population from having to travel toward a distant teaching hospital;

– a project to set up a platform for remote radiology support, on the scale of rural health consortia, in order to pool human resources (radiologists and technicians) for continued care.

I also remember a speech made by a director of the Aube CPAM (National health insurance office) in 2014, which urged health professionals, and especially hospitals, to "spend better, develop initiatives that make it possible to limit how much a patient has to travel, for reasons of economy and comfort". I will return, further on, to the development of telemedicine and the increasingly stronger links being established between medicine and information systems.

2.2.7. *Area 7*

Launched in the context of investing in the future and endowed with 80 million euros, the "territoire de soins numérique" ("digital healthcare regions") project aimed to modernize the healthcare system by experimenting, in certain pilot zones, with the most innovative health services and technologies.

The five projects chosen in September 2014 were:

– for the Aquitaine region: XL ENS (Landes espace numérique de santé [Landes digital health space]);

– for the Bourgogne region: E-TICSS (Territoire innovant coordonné santé social [Region innovating coordinated social health]);

– for the Île-de-France region: TerriS@nté (Le numérique au service de la santé en métropole du grand-Paris [Digitization to support health in the metropolis of Greater Paris]);

– for the Rhône-Alpes region: PASCALINE (Parcours de santé coordonné et accès à l'innovation numérique [Path for coordinated health and access to digital innovation]);

– for territories in the Indian ocean: PLEXUS OI (Plateforme d'échange pour les nouveaux usages des TC en santé dans l'océan Indien [Platform for exchanges on the new uses of communication technology in health in the Indian Ocean]).

However, in certain regions, such as in the Aube local health center and the local health center for the Sézanais region (which became a regional health consortium in 2016) it was decided that they would also develop a digital healthcare region project, without any dedicated financing. The project in the Aube region was called OPTIMIPSTIC, which was an acronym for "optimisation du parcours de soins grâce aux technologies de l'information et de la communication ("optimizing the care pathway using information and communication technology"). This kind of project allies principles of the DH as well as the HAS criteria with telemedicine techniques; however, the chief objective is to create a new form of governance.

The health informatics system has become a driving force and pillar of support in a new organization, new practices and in a new operational charter. The hospital IT engineer plays a major role in this, providing a link between health professionals and supervisory bodies.

2.2.8. *Area 8*

Digitization is accelerating around the world and ceaseless innovation is required to respond to the needs of healthcare professionals. Software companies do not have adequate financial resources to massively invest in R&D or to quickly develop new modules.

Resorting to in-house developments has proven to be limited in terms of durability and in terms of the integration with information systems that are constantly changing, with smaller IT teams. The solution can now be found in the implementation of framework agreements with universities.

This is, indeed, what the Troyes hospital decided to do in February 2014, entering into an agreement with the University of Technology of Troyes (UTT) focusing on innovative projects with limited budgets and the ability to bring these to life through industrial partnerships:

– RescueMap, the digitized cartography used by SAMU (the French medical emergency service) in association with the TTU and ALPIX;

– GINO, the geolocalization of patients and biomedical equipment in a hospital setting in association with the UTT and MEDASYS;

– forecasting emergency services, optimizing waiting times for emergencies with a PhD student from UTT;

– MyGHT, the secure city hospital portal;

– ALOIS, IRMA, ASMIR, IRMIS and MART, the Champagne Sud hospital robots (Figures 2.3 and 2.4).

The health informatics project chief must, today, steer this type of innovative project in order to allow their institution to optimize their IT system at the minimal cost and with results of the highest quality.

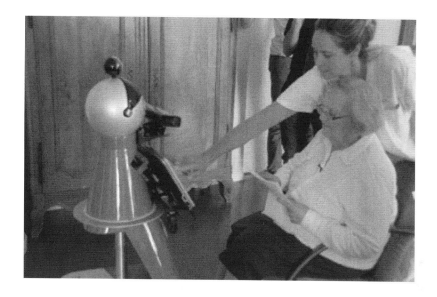

Figure 2.3. *The Champagne Sud Hospital robots. For a color version of this figure, see www.iste.co.uk/blua/hospital.zip*

To summarize these observations, we can consider that in the field of information systems today, technology is no longer a problem. Solutions and methods do exist.

Tools may be made more reliable and it is possible to ensure working continuity. The information system is open and soon we will no longer be talking about hospital informatics, but of *health* informatics.

Public powers have come to understand challenges posed by information and communication technology (ICT) and the major hurdle today lies in providing support for change, the acceptance of tools and the implementation of new systems of organization to take up the battle against medical deserts using telemedicine and a pooling of resources.

In the Troyes hospital center, for example, ICT represents two out of five focus areas of the hospital's mission plan for 2014–2018 (and all five focus areas of the Champagne Sud Hospitals are based on information technology).

Figure 2.4. *The Champagne Sud Hospital robots. For a color version of this figure, see www.iste.co.uk/blua/hospital.zip*

2.3. Information systems – communication and organization

Today, it is believed that 20% of the management of a health information system is based on technology and 80% is based on human resources. The Head of the Health Information Project becomes a veritable conductor, orchestrating the deployment and smooth functioning of the health information system, the spinal cord supporting the hospital's activities.

This can be seen throughout the organization and I propose spending a few moments studying the ideal organization of an IT and communications department. The concept of an information systems department does not really make much sense today. However, in many cases it is still an appropriate term to use, because in many hospitals the true worth of information systems is not appreciated and it remains simply a technical service, a subdivision of some functional department (often the finance department). However, if we go beyond this and attempt to speak about the department of information systems, we soon realize that the term DIS would need to be accompanied by other letters:

– an O for organization;

– a T for technology or telephony;

– a B for biomedical.

All these additions add greater meaning to the term and deserve to be brought together to form DISOTB. However, it does not really matter what we link with the information system, which depends ultimately on the context of each institution. What is most important is allying know-how and spreading knowledge – in a word, communication. And so, rather than talking about the DISOTB, more and more institutions talk about the digital informatics department, as, above all, our job consists of managing information in a digital format.

We thus begin to see the emergence of a DISC (Director of Information Systems and Communications), often in subtle ways. For example, the hiring of a "Head of Communications", whose task is to develop a website for the institution, an Intranet portal or even to manage feeds on social networks (Twitter, Facebook, LinkedIn, etc.) and specialized press.

In any case, this Head of Communication, even if they do possess alternative competencies (a background that characterizes communication) slowly becomes a sort of project manager, a catalyst, a project initiator, a worker in the shadows much like the hospital IT engineer. Similarly, the work of a Medical Informatics Director (MID) depends increasingly on a new position – the data manager, who carries out specialized tasks (SQL requests, data reconciliation and so on) to help the MID optimize coding and transmissions.

It would, thus, make sense for MID to come under the Department of Information Systems or, better yet, for both of these departments to work together. In fact, this was an observation made, recently, at meetings organized by a regional health agency (agence régionale de santé (ARS)) or the French Federation of Hospitals (FFH), since the DIM and DDI/DIS are invited together for meetings on regional reflection on the position of Director of Health Information Systems.

We will see what comes of this and allow cultures and organizations to evolve at their own pace. However, we must keep in mind that a well-organized informatics department must have close ties with, and an open mind toward, communicators (who add value to their work) and those who participate in funding and financing, whether this be the data manager of the MID or the managing director of the finance department. Regardless of your internal organization and position, always remember this when constructing the functional flow chart for hospital informatics.

2.4. Linking HIS, biomedicine and telemedicine

To conclude this chapter on the hospital and its information system, we will now return to the increasingly close ties between HIS, biomedicine and telemedicine. Here again, we offer a historical overview for an understanding of how these links have built up over time, becoming rather tenuous today and perhaps disappearing in the future. It all began with automatons in laboratories. In the 1990s, laboratory information management systems (LIMS) were the earliest "patient files" interfaced with biomedical equipment, called automatons.

We then witnessed the emergence of LIMS, which made it possible to simplify and consolidate results from connected analysis instruments, halfway between HIS and biomedicine, such as the Beckman Coulter Remisol (Mabiotech 2017) and expert systems for automatic validation, such as the Valab softtware, which is an increasingly common purchase in informatics departments (Valab 2017).

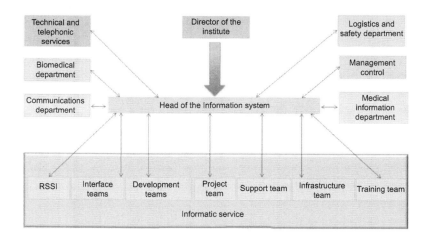

Figure 2.5. *A functional flowchart for hospital informatics*

If these systems are largely outdated today, hospital IT teams must not hesitate to solicit the help of the biomedical team (especially if they report to the same management, in the framework of a DISBD). This is because:

– it is the biomedical department that buys automatons and invoices;

– they must consider ordering a 1/2 interface on the automaton side (further, the HIPC (Chef du projet informatique hospitalier – Hospital IT project manager)must list all the 1/2 interfaces for LIMS when they draw up the CCTP (Cahier des clauses techniques particulières – Book of particular case clauses) in conjunction with biologists to ensure nothing has been forgotten).

The next development was the arrival of various imaging techniques. This ushered in the radiology information systems (RIS), which were used:

– not only to manage the workflow of the imaging services (patient arrival, quotation, interpretation, report etc.);

– but, above all, to generate the DICOM worklist: a list of patients structured in the DICOM (Digital Imaging and Communications in Medicine) format, which was then communicated to the imaging system (scanner, magnetic resonance imaging (MRI), echocardiogram, etc.) to facilitate the identification of the images produced and to consider how to archive them using identity-monitoring procedures (we will return to this later when discussing PACS).

Today, we find three types of RIS in France:

– the RIS developed by biomedical manufacturers (such as CareStream);

– independent RIS such as Xplore from EDL (the current French leader in this field);

– EPR RIS modules such as Dx Image by Medasys (a module of Dx Care).

RIS today play a major regional role in the field of health (in the context of teleradiology) and, these days, it is no longer considered by itself but coupled with a PACS (which we will return to further on). For more information on this, I invite the reader to refer to a pedagogic article published by the French Radiology Society on RIS and PACS (SFR).

Then there came the PACS. The RIS, like the LIMS, were deployed by hospital IT services but could only be used with the help of the biomedicine department, especially when they were coupled with the PACS. In addition to archiving and transmitting images, the PACS also received the DICOM worklist from the RIS and made it possible to manage the archiving of the images produced by imaging techniques, while enabling the sharing of these images across the computers on the HIS. It thus became a real interface between HIS and biomedicine based on the well-known DICOM format. PACS was increasingly implemented by the IT department. The hospital IT engineer had to link in the biomedical service to list available imaging techniques and would then verify that these were DICOM compatible and establish the cost of putting in place the interface between the PACS and each eligible imaging technique. Given the success of PACS, will other disciplines, such as nuclear medicine, maternity health and angiograms, also enter the market? The sharing of images to different departments in the hospital is a task that is not solely associated with radiology.

We find images produced in the disciplines cited above as well:

– in maternity health/gynecology (images produced by DICOM compatible ultrasound scanners via systems such as GE Healthcare's Viewpoint (GE Healthcare 2017));

– in angiography (via specific software such as CardioReport by CVX Médical (Cardio Report Storage));

– or in nuclear medicine (images produced by gamma camera via software such as Venus (Venus explorer 2017)).

And for all non-DICOM-compatible images, the PACS manufacturers offer dicomizers, which are used, for example, with images produced in surgical units (video from endoscopy carried out by urological departments and so on). One of the current market leaders in dicomization is the ETIAM dicomizer.

One of the departments that has the strongest link between HIS and biomedicine is the resuscitation unit. Resuscitation has seen biomedical interfaces peak. The resuscitation information management system interfaces with the syringe pumps, monitors and respirators. The IT project manager certainly requires the help of the biomedical team in order to successfully put in place these interfaces.

One of the market leaders in this field is Clinisoft from GE Healthcare.

As the reader must have understood by now, the HIS-biomedicine link gradually expanded and took over the entire hospital from the 1990s onward and toward the late 2010s. It was seen that this system would make it possible to open up the hospital outwards using teleradiology. Implementing PACS made it possible to consider other uses:

– a health institution has imaging techniques, radiographers but no radiologists. The institution can use a secure network to transmit its DICOM images toward a specialized center (a support hospital in the regional health consortium, for example), which will upload these images into their PACS and have them interpreted by their radiologists, subsequently sharing their reports through a secure messaging system or a secure image portal (for example, the teleradiology network set up between the Bourbonne-les-Bains hospital center and the Troyes hospital center in 2013);

– in a health institution that produces images but does not always have radiologists (a perennial problem in healthcare) and cannot store the images in accordance with regulations. This establishment can then interface its RIS and imaging techniques permanently with the PACS of a support establishment, which will not only take care of the regulatory archiving of images, but will also interpret them when the first institution does not have a radiologist available (for example, the Aube Marne Hospital Consortium imaging unit linked with the PACS of the Troyes hospital center). We then speak of a "sprawling" or "tentacular" PACS, as the PACS from the central support establishment will extend to the establishment requesting help, even transmitting images to workstations in specific units in the connected establishment. In the case of an RHC (regional hospital consortium), the PACS contains a system of reconciliation of images and grouping of identities in order to allow radiologists to view all the images of the same patient, produced in multiple establishments. It also makes it possible to consider outsourcing a part of the interpretation in a process called external tele-interpretation.

These new forms of architecture make it possible to imagine on-call teleradiology systems. Also, companies such as CTR, TELECONSUT France and ETIAM have specialized in services of this kind in order to help hospitals sustain radiology activity with fewer radiologists.

From now on, telemedicine practices will only get more and more democratized, especially with France's national mission for fighting against strokes and the development of the tele-stroke networks. The tele-stroke network, largely developed over the last 5 years, has made it possible to compensate for the absence of a neurovascular unit in certain rural health centers. This health policy made it possible to develop several tele-stroke cubicles within ER units: a soundproofed room with appropriate lighting, equipped with an HD camera and a workflow management software (with scoring) that is linked to the hospital LIMS and PACS.

This unit allows data to be transmitted in record time to an expert neurologist based in a neurovascular unit in another hospital that could be as far away as 200 km, giving them all the information required to take the right decision concerning the patient's state of health (whether this is or is not a stroke, prescribing fibrinolysis, etc.) with perfect digital traceability (and hence, responsibility).

After this, emergency telemedicine also developed (for health units and nursing homes for the elderly). It was on the basis of the tele-stroke network and other specific telemedicine projects (such as following up on wounds through telemedicine – the regional digital health spaces and the Domoplaies project, developed to treat complicated wounds) that long-term telemedicine solutions have been developed using structured software (workflow manager). Accelis Vepro and Covalia are two of the most widely used programs in France.

Today, these programs are being considered for running emergency telemedicine and giving SAMU (the French medical emergency service) new "eyes":

– a nurse in a prison health unit calls SAMU in the middle of the night as an inmate is feeling unwell: videos and connected objects (pulse, ECG, etc.) will make it possible to decide whether or not to remove the inmate from the prison;

– a nurse in a nursing home calls SAMU as an elderly resident is experiencing uneasiness: the telemedical doctor's kit, trolley and, soon, the robot that will also bring in video and transmit vital statistics to the SAMU doctor, all come into play. The doctor can then decide whether or not to deploy the resuscitation unit or to guide the State-certified nurse in providing care to the elderly patient.

These new uses and the rapid success of their implementation will soon open up the field to greater mobility, the need to provide greater access to information systems at home for patients (HAD – hospitalisation à domicile, hospitalization at home, and SSIAD – service de soins infirmiers à domicile, nursing team for care at home) and toward the advent of connected objects, which are the subject of any number of media reports. Practices have changed and the psychological barrier between biomedicine and HIS has almost disappeared ("almost" because these are still often two different fields managed by two different departments).

We are also seeing the large-scale development of applications for smartphones or tablets that make it possible to collect biomedical data and integrate them into EPRs. There is, notably, the Medasys Dx SMA system coupled with the Dx Care DPI (electronic patient records), or again the Dx HAD/SSIAD smartphone application coupled with systems that automatically collect information on vital parameters, documents, care plans, etc.

Under these conditions and with the variety of data sources external to the HIS (whether from within or outside the hospital), we can see the emergence of systems for monitoring and acquiring data remotely and the term SCADA (Supervisory Control and Data Acquisition) has been now included in the vocabulary of health information systems.

This is, however, one of the sources of worry for IT engineers, as these systems are very vulnerable to hacking. Indeed, I would like to conclude this chapter on hospital information systems by highlighting the importance of the security of health information systems (which could be the subject of an entire book and which has become a prerequisite for PHN (Programme hopital numérique–Digital hospital program), HAS and account certification) and by inviting the reader to learn more about the importance of security in the field of SCADA (Silicon 2015; Usine digitale 2017; Informatique 2017).

2.5. Conclusion

Information technology has slowly, but steadily, occupied a larger and larger space in the evolution of hospital processes. Today, its potential is fully recognized by hospital directors and is the subject of legislation under the term "health information systems". It has become an *intra-* and *inter-*hospital workflow management tool, as well as a means for communicating between hospitals in a regional healthcare consortium. Managing this tool is still a problematic process, given the lack of adequate human and financial resources, however it is seen today as the foundation for at least eight pillars to promote cooperation and quality in healthcare. With the increase in health information systems, the boundary between this and communication is slowly being erased (information-sharing helping to disseminate know-how) just as the border between the information services and biomedical services is slowly disappearing (to form more holistic technical services). The best example of this new form of cooperation is that of telemedicine, a flagship e-health project. However, given these disappearing boundaries and the optimization of the care journey through ICT, there is the evident need, now more than ever before, of prioritizing the security of information networks.

2.6. References

Agence régionale de Santé. (2017). FIDES [Online]. Available: http://www.ars. champagne-ardenne.sante.fr/fileadmin/CHAMPAGNE-ARDENNE/ARS_ Internet/actualites/Actus_2013/FIDES/DRIFP_FIDES.pdf [Accessed September 2018].

Anap. (2017). Architecture et urbanisation des sytèmes d'information de production de soins [Online]. Available: http://www.anap.fr/publications-et-outils/publications/detail/actualites/architecture-et-urbanisation-des-systemes-dinformation-de-production-de-soins/ [Accessed September 2018].

CVX Medical. (2017). Cardio report storage [Online]. Available: http://www.
    cvxmedical.com/?codepage=produits_solutions|cr_storage [Accessed September
    2018].

Degoulet, P., Marin, L., Kleinebreil, L. Albiges, B. (2003). *Présent et avenir des
    systèmes d'information et de communication hospitaliers.* Springer, Berlin.

Direction départementale des finances publiques des Côtes d'Armor. (2017). Fiche
    protocoles d'échanges standard [Online]. Available: http://www.amf22.asso.fr/
    fileadmin/users/amf22/documentation/DGFiP/PES/Fiche_PES_AMF.pdf
    [Accessed September 2018].

Etiam. (2017). Solution de gestion Dicom : etiam dicomizer [Online]. Available:
    http://www.etiam.fr/solution-de-gestion-dicom/etiam-dicom-izer/   [Accessed
    September 2018].

GE Healthcare. (2017). Solutions informatiques pour l'échographie [Online].
    Available: http://www3.gehealthcare.fr/fr-fr/products/categories/echographie/
    solutions_informatiques_pour_l_echographie/viewpoint_5 [Accessed September
    2018].

Haute autorité de Santé. (2017). Certification des logiciels d'aide à la prescription
    LAP, un premier logiciel à usage hospitalier certifié [Online]. Available: http://
    www.has-sante.fr/portail/jcms/c_1754531/fr/certification-des-logiciels-daide-a-
    la-prescription-lap-un-premier-logiciel-a-usage-hospitalier-certifie   [Accessed
    September 2018].

Himss Europe. (2017). Healthcare information and management systems society
    [Online]. Available: http://www.himss.eu/ [Accessed September 2018].

Informatique. (2017). Vulnérabilité des sytèmes scada [Online]. Available:
    http://www.informatiquenews.fr/vulnerabilite-systemes-scada-jean-pierre-carlin-
    logrhythm-5739 [Accessed September 2018].

Mabiotech. (2017). Remisol advance, systèmes d'informations cliniques [Online].
    Available: http://www.mabiotech.com/details-remisol+advance+systemes+d+
    informations+clinique+beckman+coulter-68.html [Accessed September 2018].

Ministère de la Santé. (2017). Financement des établissements de santé
    [Online]. Available: http://www.sante.gouv.fr/financement-des-etablissements-de-
    sante,6619.html [Accessed September 2018].

Ministère de la Santé. (2017). Projet FIDES, rapport au parlement [Online].
    Available: http://www.sante.gouv.fr/IMG/pdf/Projet_FIDES_Rapport_au_
    Parlement.pdf [Accessed September 2018].

Nicesoft. (2017). Venus explorer [Online]. Available: http://www.nice-soft.fr/fr/
    venus-explorer-processing/ [Accessed September 2018].

Ponçon, G. (2000). Le management du système d'information hospitalier : la fin de la dictature technologique. École nationale de la santé publique, Rennes.

SFR. (2017). Portail de la radiologie [Online]. Available: http://www.sfrnet.org/Data/upload/Images/COM [Accessed September 2018].

Silicon. (2015). Sécurité des scada : pourquoi la côte d'alerte est atteinte [Online]. Available: http://www.silicon.fr/securite-des-scada-pourquoi-la-cote-dalerte-est-atteinte-107620.html.

Télésanté Basse Normandie. (2017). L'ENRS et les projets domoplaies [Online]. Available: http://www.telesante-basse-normandie.fr/l-enrs-et-les-projets/domoplaies,1641,2503.html [Accessed September 2018].

Université de technologie de Troyes. (2017). Systèmes d'information et logistiques hospitaliers [Online]. Available: http://exed.utt.fr/fr/formations-courtes-professionnalisantes/diplome-universite/diplome-universite-systemes-d-information-et-logistiques-hospitaliers.html [Accessed September 2018].

Usine digitale. (2017). La sécurité des réseaux scada : un enjeu national [Online]. Available: http://www.usine-digitale.fr/article/la-securite-des-reseaux-scada-un-enjeu-national.N273662 [Accessed September 2018].

Valab. (2017). [Online]. Available: http://www.valab.com/index.phpoption=com_content&view=article&id=83&Itemid=134) [Accessed September 2018].

Wikipedia. (2017). Objectif national des dépenses d'assurance maladie [Online]. Available: http://fr.wikipedia.org/wiki/Objectif_national_des_depenses_d'assurance_maladie [Accessed September 2018].

Wikipedia. (2018a). Digital imaging and communications in medicine [Online]. Available: https://fr.wikipedia.org/wiki/ Digital_ imaging_and_communications_in_medicine [Accessed September 2018].

Wikipedia. (2018b). Supervisory control and data acquisition [Online]. Available: https://fr.wikipedia.org/wiki/Supervisory_Control_and_Data_Acquisition [Accessed September 2018].

Medical Informatics: Historical Overview, Supports and Challenges

3.1. Introduction

Medical informatics is a field that emerged in France in the 1980s with the arrival of the Program to Medicalize Information Systems (PMIS). Directly inspired by the American model of modulating healthcare financing, the French program followed a different logic in the French health system. The goal was to use the PMIS as an epidemiological tool and also as a tool for budget allocations. Institutions were required to analyze their activity (law of July 31, 1991) and this resulted in the structuring of medical information, which is today a major support in the invoicing of hospital stays. In parallel, information in health institutions can be obtained from various sources today.

Some of these are directly linked to patient care, whereas others are linked with the management and administration of hospital facilities. These components play an important role today in the context of the multidisciplinary approach to research into the performance of systems and organizations.

There are multiple and varied sources of information, from paper tools to data, that are structured through digital processing. In this context, the challenge that arises is that of being able to make use of routine data in order to propose indicators for steering decisions and for surveillance. The digital

Chapter written by David LAPLANCHE and Stéphane SANCHEZ.

transition of these different components is, therefore, a major challenge that must be resolved to improve human and financial management of health institutions. The structure and quality of the tools play an essential role in using data, as we will see through theoretical discussion as well as concrete examples.

3.2. Information sources

3.2.1. *Data that can be used in the hospital sector*

Information in the hospital sector is obtained from several data sources. The primary sources are administrative data and patient-related data (Figure 3.1).

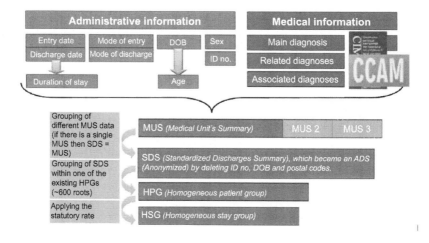

Figure 3.1. *Data gathered for invoicing a hospital stay*

3.2.1.1. *Administrative data*

A large amount of administrative data are generated within a hospital: data relating to staff, equipment, purchases and maintenance, finances and accounting, etc. All of this information is stored by institutions according to their archival rules. Paper-based records were the norm for a long time and it is difficult to routinely use the data from these for studies, either because of the difficulty in referring to the handwritten notes or the need to constantly return to the paper documents when referring to data.

The implementation of cost accounting and the arrival of certification of accounts and work based on the performance of a health institution sensitized management to the benefits of informatics tools to easily make use of the data collected.

3.2.1.2. *Patient-related data*

There are two kinds of patient-related data: administrative and medical. While the amount and quality of data collected vary from institution to institution, some of them are common across sites as they are mandatory in the context of the financing of stays and are defined within a legal framework.

For example, administrative data offer a complete overview of the patient's identity, their data of birth, how they entered the institution and where they came from, as well as their discharge from the institution and where they are going next, etc.

Medical data include different diagnostics, the medical actions carried out during the patient's stay, any high-cost medication administered (e.g. chemotherapy) as well as any expensive equipment that was used (e.g. pacemaker and prosthesis). Along with this mandatory information, a variety of data are available more or less easily on different media: in the patient file, for example. Depending on the medium, the data will be more or less structured and usable.

3.2.2. *Different media*

Today, medical information is stored chiefly in two formats: paper and digital. The coexistence of both these formats makes the use of data quite complicated, as retrieving data might be a lengthy process and may include several uncertainties.

Paper records have, historically, been widely used in medicine. However, the quality and legibility of these records have often been denounced on several grounds: quality of writing, lack of standardization of the information they contain, loss of some sections of a file and so on. These paper records are often scattered within an institution and this makes it difficult to access and use their contents. Archives, thus, play a primordial role in collecting and unifying all components in a file, but unfortunately, older forms of organization and individual attitudes complicate or derail this process.

Aside from the patient records, there are a number of other sources of information that are available. As these are often collective (i.e. they concern several patients), these data cannot be entered into a single patient file and are, therefore, difficult to use. These include, for example, information on handrails, on schedules, files on the traceability of toxins, etc.

Information technology, today, seems the most appropriate tool for making use of data. However, it is not free of flaws. Indeed, the large number of software programs, each with a different architecture and with interfacing not always possible between them (or being very time consuming), frequently makes it very complicated to collect information. And this is where we find the most difficult challenge to a successful transition to a digital system: generating reliable, structured, reproducible, interoperable and, thus, usable data, all while taking into account the user who will be entering this information in order to simplify this task for them and, therefore, to make it more easily accepted.

3.2.3. *Legal framework*

3.2.3.1. *The general framework*

While the goal here is to collect the maximum amount of data that can be used for analysis, there is, nonetheless, a strict legal framework that guarantees the confidentiality of all data collected.

The medical information contained in the patient records is subject to strict legislative rules. Law no. 2002-303, dated March 4, 2002, gave greater clarity on to what constitutes the patient file (art. R1112-2 of the Public Health Code for France) by defining three broad areas of content:

– formalized information collected during outpatient consultations in the institution, at the time of admitting a patient into the emergency services, or at the time of admission and during a hospital stay (reasons for hospitalization, medical history, medical observations, etc.);

– formalized information established at the end of the patient's stay in hospital (hospitalization report, discharge letter, prescription, manner of discharge, etc.);

– any information stating it was collected from third parties who did not participate in the therapeutic care or about such third parties (e.g. medical students).

3.2.3.2. *Archives*

The broad rules governing the archiving of medical information do not depend on the format in which the information is stored, but on the person concerned. With regard to the time frame for conserving this information, the records of patients who are adults can be conserved for 20 years, starting from the most recent stay or visit by the patient to the hospital. For minors, this period may go beyond 20 years, as the information may be conserved until the person turns 28 years old. For patients who have undergone a transfusion or patients who have been tested in the context of a postmortem organ donation, the information may be preserved for 30 years. Finally, for deceased patients, information may be saved for 10 years postmortem (art. R1112-7 of the public health code for France). At the end of the designated period, the files are destroyed, as per article L212-2 of the heritage code, by the archivist, after agreement between whoever bears legal responsibility (the hospital director) and the Medical Information Department (MID) (which is responsible for the confidentiality of this information).

3.2.3.3. *Rules of confidentiality*

Medical information deals with sensitive data whose processing is governed by legislation. The primary article that discusses confidentiality is article L1110-4:

"Any person who is given care by a healthcare professional, institution or service, a professional or organization working towards prevention or administering care and whose activities are governed by the present code, the health service in the armed forces, a professional from the medico-social or social sector or an institution of social service or medico-social service mentioned in I of article L312-1 of the Families and Social Action code has the right to have their privacy respected and to keeping confidential any information concerning this private life..." (art. L1110-4).

This confidentiality makes data on health, as well as accessing these data, a very sensitive affair on a legal level. These components first of all necessitate the storage and protections of these data in dedicated locations that are well secured (for paper documents) or on protected servers (for digital documents).

By its very function, the MID benefits from certain derogations to these rules. Practitioners working within these institutions share the nominative medical data that are required for analyzing activity and for invoicing with the MID doctor who is in charge of medical information for the institution, following conditions that have been laid down in an official act. The data collected in the context of the PMIS are, therefore, protected by professional confidentiality (art. L1110-4 and R4127-4 of the Public Health Code, article 226-13 of the Penal Code, article 4 of the Medical Deontology Code). It is, thus, mandatory for a doctor to be in charge of MID and as a result, the medical data collected by MID are also covered by the confidentiality clause that governs any doctor–patient relationship. In parallel to these legislative measures, the Data Protection and Freedom of Information Law (dated January 6, 1978) was added to the provisions of the public health code that dealt with data related to health.

3.2.3.4. *Data Protection and Freedom of Information – the future* data protection officer

Since 2004, institutions have been given the choice of designating someone to be in charge of Data Protection and Freedom of Information, whose role, within the institution, will be that of promoting respect for the law. As concerns medical information, their role is limited, as this department is managed by other actors. However, this person will be in charge of ensuring that in everyday matters the rights of patients are respected in the context of their right to access their personal data. This role changed in May 2018, with the arrival of the General European Regulations on Data Protection, which transformed this role, with the official designation DPO (data protection officer). This required a greater collaboration between medical information, management and the DPO in the context of respecting and protecting data on health.

3.2.4. *Digital transition*

3.2.4.1. *The transition to the digital format*

The digital transition poses a number of challenges to health institutions, many of which revolve around the efficiency of the existing structures. However, there are also challenges in responding to new norms.

For example, health establishments are now subject to quality certification. This process was put in place in order to incentivize hospitals to offer high-quality care throughout a region. To obtain this certification, the institutions must provide proof of actions that have been implemented. Traceability is, therefore, a major challenge in this process and computerization proved an important aid here, even though it did generate new challenges in terms of data security and data use.

Similarly, institutions whose budget exceeds a threshold of 100 million euros are subject to the annual certification of their financial budgets. As with the quality certification, bringing in these added elements is the institution's responsibility. The structure and availability of the data are, therefore, essential in order to be able to respond to any comments raised by the auditors.

Finally, to return to the legal aspects and the quality of the care given to the patient, it seems crucial that the different actions involved in a patient's stay are traced and stored, so that they may be referred to if the patient has any questions. This is not only for legal actions, but will also be useful for future admissions in order to better understand the patient's history and allow a practitioner to get a better overall picture of the patient.

3.2.4.2. *Financial support*

In a context where financial budgets are tight, the State must support these institutions. This has been the case for several programs such as the Digital Hospital Programme, started in 2011, which offers financial support to the health sector for computerization. Through this, institutions receive aid in the start-up phase. The remainder of the money is only transferred once the project goals for that institution are achieved.

The regional program for digital care, launched in 2014 in the context of future investments and endowed with 80 million euros, aims to modernize the healthcare system by experimenting, in certain pilot zones, with the latest and most innovative services and technology in e-health.

The final and most recent example is the National e-Health Strategy 2020, whose goal is to support actors in the healthcare systems in making the digital shift and allow France to remain at the cutting edge of innovation. Along with these grand plans, several targeted actions have been undertaken, such as the computerization of emergency departments. Concrete examples of these are discussed later on.

3.2.4.3. *Factors slowing down the transition*

While the stakes are clear, both in qualitative as well as financial terms, there are several factors that are slowing down this digital transition. Despite the State's support across the board for these grand plans, the financing is not exhaustive and in order to benefit from available financing, institutions must provide documentation that may be very complex. The balance amount that they must put in may sometimes dissuade them or hamper projects because of the initial investment required, while certain projects may provide no direct financial returns once implemented.

Along with these financial considerations, we must also highlight the difficulty in getting members of the nursing staff to adhere to this digital transition. Indeed, the culture of paper files is still very strong in this milieu, regardless of whether one is a medical or paramedical professional. The computerization of paramedical services has sometimes had to be carried out coercively but an established hierarchy ensured that this change was pushed through. It is a different story when it comes to medical teams. While the generation-gap or "cultural factor" argument may be used, this is not enough to explain the glacial speed at which IT solutions have been deployed. The resistance to change in this field is very strong and there are many arguments that have been put forth against the transition. To accelerate the speed at which people comply with the change, institutions must leverage willing practitioners who can then demonstrate the added value and the benefits that computerization can offer, such as the direct access to patient data and their history, the ease of consulting these data and the possibility of rapidly generating a report. There must be significant support both in terms of software use as well as for hardware. Mobile tools improve acceptance. Having ergonomic software and hardware is, therefore, fundamental. It is also essential to ensure that the data entered are as comprehensive as possible in order to use it in the same way that we used the data in our work with the ER services.

3.3. Using information

The multiple sources of data and the progressive streamlining of these sources have made it possible to use the data for multiple purposes. Three examples are discussed below in detail: PMIS, which is, today, essential for the funding of institutions; the use of research that contributes to improving medical practices; and a concrete case that also serves as an introduction to the following chapter on the computerization of an ER unit.

3.3.1. *PMIS*

3.3.1.1. *Historical overview and evolution*

The PMIS, the programme to medicalize information systems, was introduced in France in 1982. The goal of this program was to collect all information relating to a patient's stay in hospital: administrative data as well as medical data (diagnosis, actions carried out, etc.). Collecting this information was, initially, optional, with the goal being that of epidemiological research and gaining an understanding of hospital activity. It became mandatory in 1991 (the Law dated July 31, 1991; articles L6113-7 and L6113-8 of the Public Health Code) and has, since, become an important tool in establishing tariffs for hospital stays in the context of the "price per activity" system in 2005.

The challenges related to these data have, thus, evolved considerably and the PMIS has often been the gateway for computerization in hospitals. Note that 35 years after this program was introduced, it has become an established strategic tool. The quality and optimization of the data gathered through PMIS makes it possible to improve revenue as well as manage performance through specific studies (studying opportunities, market shares, profitability, etc.) to develop activities and strategy. On a larger scale, it makes it possible to carry out a reflection on hospital activity, health of citizens and the resulting costs.

The difficulty in gathering information lies in the variety of sources for the data. Administrative and medical data for a stay are rarely from the same software. Ensuring that these formats are interoperable and similar is essential in order to be able to establish connections between the data in order to link it up and send it to the supervisory bodies in the format that they require.

3.3.1.2. *MID*

MIDs were established in 1989. These departments aim to centralize information obtained through the PMIS in order to be able to transmit them to management. An MID is managed by a hospital doctor. Depending on the hospital, MID may be organized as a centralized service or a decentralized one.

The decentralized MIDs collect information on the codes for the medical actions and diagnoses carried out by professionals on the ground and then proceed to review these before sending them. Centralized MIDs bring together the different data on hospital stays, proceed to assign codes to each piece of information and then review them before sending them. This organization is based on professionals who can assign the correct codes (secretaries, paramedics and so on).

The role of MIDs varied from hospital to hospital for a long time. The Health Law of 2016 made it possible to clarify this role through the implementation of the regional healthcare consortia, which were functional support groups between several health establishments located within the same region (supporting each other in the MID, purchases, convergent information systems, etc.). The emergence of these regional MIDs, therefore, required that the role of an MID be clearly defined. Thus, from 2016 onwards the goals of an MID have been arranged along four main axes:

– organizing the production of medical data and the evaluation of the quality and transmission of these data in close collaboration with the invoicing chain;

– medical analysis of hospital activity and providing strategic and medico-economic expertise;

– designing and contributing to the development of administrative and clinical information systems, systems for managing confidentiality and contributing to policies on the protection and the management of medical archives;

– designing and/or contributing to clinical research projects, as well as research into epidemiology, health informatics and medico-economic research.

3.3.1.3. *Analysis tools*

Through their mission objectives, MID doctors become essential actors in hospital strategy in the development of information systems and the structuring of data. To achieve the stated objectives, they must equip themselves with high-performing tools to input, extract and analyze data. These tools depend on making use of the data being transmitted to the supervisory bodies and also on other sources such as INSEE (France's National Institute of Statistics and Economic Studies). A few examples of how these are used are given below.

The medico-economic analysis tools are often employed in MIDs. The goal is to make use of all the activity data that are transmitted on a monthly basis to the supervisory bodies. These tools make it possible to access the data aggregated over several years (longitudinal studies): the sector-wise evolution of activity, comparative analyses within the same institution or benchmarking this with respect to other institutions, tracking financial accounts, flagging atypical data and so on. These software have now become an integral part of hospital strategy and make it possible to optimally follow the dynamism and potential for change within institutions.

Along with these preadjusted tools, health institutions also require statistical tools in order to be able to describe and analyze all the data presented in the information system. The variety of databases require that they be perfectly structured in order to be best studied. The studies may have multiple objectives, ranging from the simple study of the activity of one healthcare professional to the compilation of the entire data set for a sector, such as the surgical unit, in order to contribute to the restructuring of this sector and the optimization of its functioning. The quality, format, availability and structure of the database are all, therefore, essential for efficiently handling requests and for the "support objective" of the projects.

Access to certain tools, such as the tool developed by ARS Île de France (Agence régionale de santé – Regional health agency), the software platform DIAMANT, makes it possible to offer the most appropriate response by decompartmentalizing information produced by different partner institutions of the ARS at a national level and allowing users to rapidly respond to *ad hoc* request related to the new regional challenges. Other online tools, especially on the ATIH Scan Santé platform, also make it possible to fill out this information.

3.3.2. *Medical information in research*

Today, the data from medical information represent a historical administrative group of data that are ambispective and very useful to a regulator as well as to actors on the ground in three specific areas. The data represent what is today considered to be routinely produced data and it is their potential use in epidemiology and surveillance of health that we will describe here. In the first place, at the epidemiological level and linked together with the database from SNIIRAM (France's national inter-regime information system for medical insurance), it makes it possible to evaluate the care paths and the administration of care. This, for example, is the approach that was used in the context of the Médiator® scandal (a weight-loss drug that led to hundreds of deaths and was the subject of a long-drawn legal battle in France, where the State was held culpable in one judgment and the company, Servier, forced to take full responsibility in another judgment with a different plaintiff. Some hearings are still ongoing in 2019). These data were used to evaluate the health impact the drug had on patients by chaining together data on consumption by town, long-term effects and history of visits to the hospital along with their diagnoses. In this case, medical information made it possible to quickly and easily quantify a large-scale medical phenomenon.

In the second place, a routine database at a national level contributes to the improvement of the quality of care provided, as can be seen in the work carried out by John E. Wennberg in *Tracking Medicine* (Wennberg 2010), who pioneered the geographic approach with respect to American databases and whose work contributed greatly to the improvement and standardization of surgical care throughout the region. Indeed, this is the approach that is being carried out in France today, as we can see in the projects undertaken by IRDES (the Institute of Research and Documentation in the Economics of Health) in 2016 in the *Atlas des variations de pratiques médicales en France* (Atlas of Variations in Medical Practices in France) (IRDES 2016). The work carried out by HAS on postsurgical thrombosis in orthopedics, inspired by the Patient Safety Indicators (Rivard 2005), also fits into this framework of using routinely produced medical information to improve and homogenize care practices. Finally, the PMIS is also a potential resource to improve patient screening, particularly in hospitals, and especially in the case of rare diseases, as it makes it possible to signpost patient profiles based on information from past inpatient hospital stays. This approach makes it possible to have a more reliable vision, on the ground, of an institution's ability to ensure precise recruitment.

Medical information in hospitals thus plays a key role in current approaches, both as concerns research into health systems (quality, safety, performance) as well as in terms of practical efficiency in carrying out high-quality clinical research.

3.3.3. *Structure and use: an example from an ER unit*

3.3.3.1. *Organization of emergency units*

Emergency units are hospital (or private) services that accept non-scheduled consultations in an institution. These services must ensure that a patient is admitted irrespective of the origin of their pathology (24/7). These services form a territorial grid in order to respond to the needs of the population.

This availability, combined with medical desertification and the possibility of carrying out all the necessary examinations in a single site, results in a marked increase in the number of people coming into these sites. At present, this increase is, on average, 3% per year but may be as high as 10% based on the structures and local situations.

3.3.3.2. *The computerization of emergency units*

The computerization of emergency care units has become a necessity for several reasons. As the number of records is constantly increasing due to the increased number of visits, it has become difficult to manage paper documents. The quality of care given is also brought into question. Then again, some patients often need to visit the same department for consultations several times a year (either because their illness requires it or for routine visits). To improve care, it is important to have access to the patient's history, that is, to the reports from their previous consultations. The constant flow of patients into the emergency unit does not make it easy to access paper archives and computerization made it possible to make this information available in real time.

Computerization was also mandatory for these services as the regional health agencies developed observatories to which the units were obliged to make reports on their daily activities via the RPU (*résume de passage aux urgences*, summary of the emergency visit).

This summary has been standardized and contains information that can be reported in each consultation. The summary has been made mandatory through an order dated July 24, 2013 and contains medical, administrative and demographic data from each visit to the emergency unit. This summary is then forwarded for analysis, as can be seen in the flowchart in Figure 3.2.

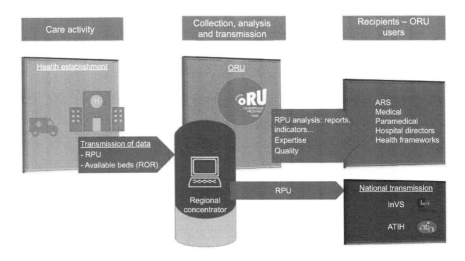

Figure 3.2. *Collection and sharing of emergency visit summaries in Champagne-Ardenne (source: www.oru-ca.com)*

This structure allowed these units to be able to gain a panoramic view of their activities and depending on the software solution that was chosen and the structure of the data base (if this existed) to make use of this data themselves for different studies.

It is the high quality of this database that made it possible to carry out the different studies presented further on in this book at the Troyes hospital center. Thus, a mandatory regulation was used to generate organizational changes.

3.4. Conclusion

The structuring of medical information has accelerated in the past 30 years due to the various challenges (epidemiological, financial, organizational and strategic) that surround the improvement of performance. The emergence of departments of medical information supported this process without, however, standardizing it. The MID landscape is, indeed, quite a heterogeneous one, which depends on the institutions within which they operate. The Health Law of 2016 and the creation of regional MIDs today makes it possible to better define the framework and the organization of MIDs in day-to-day activities, leading to continuous improvement in the quality of the medical information produced. To conclude, the relationship between the MID and the information system appears, today, to be essential and indispensable at a time when the hospital world is making a digital shift. The MID works as quality control, while the information systems are actors that implement a high-performing tool within the institutions. Collaboration between these departments is, thus, the cornerstone in helping institutions produce structured data that are easily accessible, and thus can be efficiently used by the various tools available today to process these data.

3.5. References

IRDES (2016). Atlas des variations de pratiques médicales. Recours à dix interventions chirurgicales [Online]. Available: http://www.irdes.fr/recherche/ouvrages/002-atlas-des-variations-de-pratiques-medicales-recours-a-dix-interventions-chirurgicales.pdf.

Payet, C., Polazzi, S., Lifante, J.C., Cotte, E., Obadia, J.F. Carty, M.J., Sanchez, S., Duclos, A. (2018). Influence of trends in hospital volume over time on patient outcomes for high-risk surgery. *J Am Coll Surg*, 227(4):e31.

Rivard, P.E., Rani Elwy, A., Loveland, S., Zhao S., Tsilimingras, D., Elixhauser, A., Romano, P.S., Rosen, K.A. (2005). *Applying Patient Safety Indicators (PSIs) Across Health Care Systems: Achieving Data Comparability. Advances in Patient Safety: From Research to Implementation (Volume 2: Concepts and Methodology)*. Agency for Healthcare Research and Quality, Rockville.

Sanchez, S., Payet, C., Lifante, J.C., Polazzi, S., Chollet, F., Carty, M.J., Duclos, A. (2015). Surgical risks associated with winter sport tourism, *PLoS One*, doi: 10.1371/journal.pone.0124644.

Wennberg, J.E. (2010). *Tracking Medicine, A Researcher's Quest to Understand Health Care*. Oxford University Press, Oxford.

4

Challenges in Hospital Logistics: the Example of the Champagne Sud Hospitals

4.1. Introduction

The hospital logistics commission of the ASLOG (French Logistics Association) defines hospital logistics as "the management of the flow of patients, products, materials, services and information relating to them, in order to ensure quality and safety meet a defined standard of performance and efficiency, from the supplier to the patient and, depending on the case, the final user". We focus here on logistical functions in a hospital in the strictest sense of the term, as defined by the Department of Purchases and Logistics of the Champgne Sud hospitals. These cover the flow of accommodation services meant for the patient and care services (food and laundry), the logistics of distribution of supplies and materials (pharmaceutical as well as non-pharmaceutical supplies) and the removal services (removal of waste, dirty linen and used crockery).

We will not be looking at the problem of patient flow, which brings its own specific set of challenges that are different from those related to the flow of materials, as are the challenges related to the flow of laboratory samples, medical files, etc., which are not "heavy" logistical flows in the manner of those discussed above.

Chapter written by Frédéric LUTZ.

These heavy logistical flows have certain features unique to the hospital world:

– a heterogeneous range of products transported (linen, pharmaceutical supplies, general supplies, food products, waste);

– an explosion in the product flow: a very large number of delivery as well as removal points, both in terms of the number of institutions in a region, as well as in the number of departments to supply/remove products from within each institutions (the departments themselves being either in the same building, as in the Troyes hospital center (HC), or in separate buildings, as in the Brienne-le-Château site of the Aube public health institution);

– strict restrictions, which are also quite varied depending on the flows being transported: round-the-year availability and a constant demand for supplies; the need for quick responses for urgent deliveries;

– varied modes of supply: out of stock and in-stock.

There are multiple challenges around these logistical functions, but they may all be broadly grouped under two heads that form a seemingly paradoxical injunction:

– ensuring supplies for the care activities of the hospitals and patients, by ensuring the continuity of supplies, while also respecting strict rules of hygiene and safety. Thus, any malfunction could have an immediate impact on the patients' safety and the quality of care provided to them. Smooth operations on this front will allow care professionals (the therapeutic team made up of doctors and other health professionals) to be freed of any responsibility for logistics;

– responding to the demands for economic performance made with respect to public health establishments in general, as well as to the demands of the rationale behind territorialization, with the implementation of regional hospital consortia. These are demands that logistical functions must also meet.

Despite this double challenge, both qualitative and economic, the organization of the institutions under the Champagne Sud hospitals responded for many years through "common sense" measures that displayed a willingness to comply with these, without really applying scientific and mathematical models to logistics, or using the appropriate software that have been widely used for years within the industry or mass-marketed software.

4.2. Challenges facing care professionals

The first challenge in hospital logistical functions is to serve as a support function that offers services to the care units. Indeed, the existence of logistical services in a hospital must make it possible to relieve care professionals of logistical tasks so that they can focus on caring for the patient. This may seem obvious, however historically the organization of hospitals, or the configuration of hospital sites, has not always allowed this ideal organization to be established.

Thus, until October 2014, in the Simone Veil hospital[1] at the Troyes HC, professionals from the care units would need to carry out a large part of the logistical tasks themselves.

They would have to go collect supply carts from the corridors and take them up to their respective departments. The logistics department would simply deposit the carts at the bottom floor of the elevator to each unit as taking them up to the unit would, in general, put too great a strain on the human resources in the logistics department.

Care professionals would also be required to remove any waste produced in their units, carrying them to collection points that were sometimes far away from the original departments, resulting in their absence from their units over long periods, which could be up to 20 minutes (see Figure 4.4, which depicts four collection points for the entire site of the Simone Veil hospital, representing a complex of about 8 hectares and 98,000 m² of area across all the buildings). Finally, the care units would also have to take charge of arranging supplies in the central store as well as pharmaceutical deliveries to reserves within their own departments[2].

In October 2014, a new hospitalization building was opened in the Simone Veil hospital, with a capacity of 430 beds, across five storeys, transferred from the older buildings. This new building allowed the care service teams transferred here to be relieved of the majority of their logistical tasks by implementing the following measures:

---

1 Known as the Hauts-Clos hospital, until 2018. It is the principal site of the HC in Troyes.
2 This putting away of supplies would take place at night.

– the installation of an automated guided heavy transport system (AGV) relieved carers of the time-consuming and thankless task of handling the waste-removal carts. Trolleys carrying food, linen, supplies and pharmaceutical products are now directly delivered to the floor corresponding to the appropriate care department by robots that are programmed to use the elevators; the trolleys that carry away dirty linen, food trolleys and trolleys carrying refuse are also automatically handled by these robots;

– the wards in the new hospitalization building are arranged such that there are three units on each floor, with an average of 30 beds each (or 90 beds overall, per floor) with common logistics sites for the whole floor.

This grouping of departments, in conjunction with the automation of tasks involving trolley deliveries, has made it possible to reorganize care-giving teams, which has resulted in a gain in job posts across care-giving teams as well as logistics teams: these posts have been redeployed to create 18 housekeeping posts.

Thus, each floor in the new building now benefits from housekeeping services all through the week, from 6.15 a.m. to 8.30 p.m[3], with a housekeeper (male or female) who carries out logistical tasks for all departments on that floor: taking charge of carts delivered by the robots; putting away the pharmaceutical products and other supplies in reserves; taking charge of the work clothes for the staff, made available in a changing room that is common to the whole floor; reheating meals and preparing the food-distribution trolleys; the centralization of orders for supplies; and carrying out the washing-up for the entire floor after a meal.

As a result of the new system of organization, there is greater availability of care-giving teams for overseeing patients: for example, it is possible to estimate that the automation of the clearing away of waste has resulted in gains that are equivalent to a total of four full-time care personnel, redistributed around patient beds[4].

---

3 There is a morning shift and an afternoon shift.
4 This does not mean that four additional posts would be created. It signifies the overall time that was gained across the services transferred to the new building, this being the total of the time saved across each team.

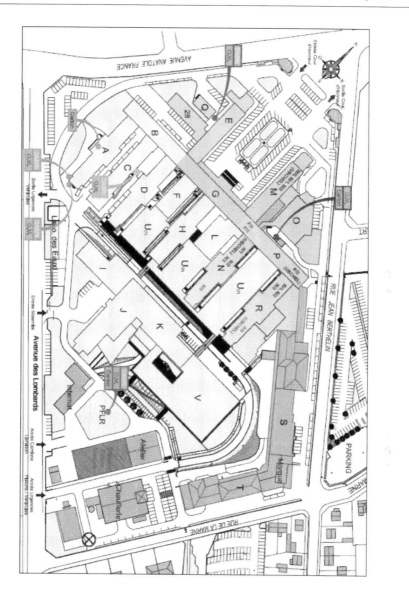

Figure 4.1. *Data collected from the invoicing of stay in a health facility. OM: the collection point for household waste; DASRI: the collection point for waste from care activities with the risk of infection. Cartons: collection point for cartons. For a color version of this figure, see www.iste.co.uk/blua/hospital.zip*

Figure 4.2. *View of the new hospitalization building*
in the Simone Veil hospital

This ability to relieve the care-giving teams of logistical tasks is coupled with an ergonomic benefit: that of helping the carers avoid the risk of work accidents or professional illnesses related to handling logistics. The profession of a caregiver is among those where the risk of musculo-skeletal problems is particularly high, related here to the handling of patients. It is, thus, advisable to spare these employees from the additional load of handling trolleys related to logistics flows, *a fortiori* for a workforce that is largely female, especially as the carts may sometimes be particularly heavy and unwieldy. For example, the trolleys delivered to the care services in the Troyes HC may be as heavy as 500 kg for those that transport pharmaceutical supplies or supplies to the central store.

Today, in institutions such as the Troyes HC, the challenge is to continue to build on this organization, which is based on housekeeping, across all care-giving departments (while also working with a constant overall number of employees) in order to relieve care-giving teams of logistics tasks.

4.3. Challenges around safety and the continuity in supplies

There can be no interruptions in supplies to various care services in the hospital. Can you imagine a surgical unit lacking clean scrubs and sterile dressings? Can you imagine not giving hospitalized patients their food? Can you imagine not changing the sheets or not removing waste that poses the risk of infection in a unit that cares for immunocompromised patients?

Figure 4.3. *An automated guided heavy transport vehicle in the Simone Veil hospital*

4.3.1. *The need for regularity in supplies*

Logistics flows in hospitals must be governed by regularity in supplies: as concerns the delivery of means, these must, of course, be provided twice a day, every day, at least for meals directly delivered from food production units[5]. Clean linen and clothing must be available to staff every day to change the sheets on the patients' beds and so they can have a new, clean uniform everyday[6], dress patients who are going in for a procedure, etc. Pharmaceutical and non-pharmaceutical deliveries must be available in sufficient quantities for the care teams.

---

5 Breakfast at the Troyes HC, for example, is not served from the central kitchen, but is prepared from produce stored within the care services and fresh bread directly delivered by the suppliers to each hospital site. For some services (the Nazareth retirement home in the Troyes HC or the majority of the public mental health facilities in Aube, for instance), meals are pre-prepared in a cold chain and one or two meals are delivered in advance to the site or the department and stored in refrigerated storage rooms.

6 With regard to weekends, for mid-size health facilities such as the Troyes HC, where laundry is delivered from Monday to Saturday, the weekly batches include a surplus that covers the weekend. In institutions where a large number of the beds are for the elderly, where the facility is a residential one rather than a care facility, the sheets need not be changed every day. In this case, each department may take delivery of clean laundry only thrice a week, with the quantity of each load being such that it will cover any requirements until the next delivery, and the changing rooms for staff are also sufficiently stocked with clean clothing.

Thus, at the Troyes HC, in the Simone Veil hospital alone (this being the main site in the hospital center, comprising around 600 beds, across buildings, for medicine, surgery and obstetric patients) the internal logistics flows represent at least 600 journeys (300 each, to and fro) for the trolleys, every single day. The flow is, of course, reduced on weekends (the absence of certain deliveries to the central store, pharmaceutical product deliveries and smaller flows of laundry), however, they remain essential (delivery of meals, urgent restocking of medication for new arrivals or for a new prescription). This need for regularity is combined with the need to adhere to distribution schedules, which are particularly strict in hospitals. Meals, for example, must be delivered at the stated hour.

For the Simone Veil hospital, for instance, meals are delivered from the Saint-Julien-les-Villas logistics center and are delivered to the hospital in refrigerated trucks. Once they arrive on the site, in order to maintain the cold chain, they must be delivered within an hour following their arrival in the intended department.

This requirement is complicated by restrictions on the size of flows and architectural restrictions. For example, meals trolleys are delivered in the Simone Veil hospital in batches of 15 trolleys, which correspond to the capacity of one delivery truck. The majority of the distribution within the Simone Veil hospital is carried out by automated guided heavy transport vehicles. The transport capacity of these is limited by the size of the fleet (11 robots) as well as the capacity of the freight elevators, which often become a site for bottlenecks in the flow. In the new building, there are three freight elevators used by the automated system and there are two in the logistics center in the Hauts-Clos hospital, where the carts can be received. There is also a gallery several hundred meters long that connects the logistic center in the Simone Veil hospital with the new building (see Figure 4.4).

Thus, in order to respond to these various demands (demands in terms of delivery deadlines, factors limiting delivery speed), logistics flows in a hospital such as the Simone Veil hospital must obey a precise sequencing. Beyond the requirements related to the prevention of the risk of food contamination, any delay in the delivery of meals could be a source of malfunctions that will negatively impact the care facility: a delay in the delivery of meal carts will result in a delay in reheating the food, which will delay the serving of meals by professionals, thus delaying all care services; a delay in meal services in a retirement home for the elderly will delay the time when professionals become available to help get the most dependent residents ready for bed, an essential and time-consuming task in a retirement home that requires the presence of the care team on the day shift, before the shift changes and the smaller team on night shift takes over.

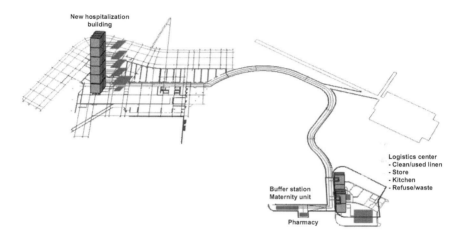

Figure 4.4. *The distribution circuit for the flow of laundry, meals, central store supplies and pharmaceutical supplies to the new hospitalization building in the Simone Veil hospital of the Troyes hospital center. For a color version of this figure, see www.iste.co.uk/blua/hospital.zip*

These challenges related to adhering to distribution schedules are complicated by the exigencies of the removal schedules. The collection of dirty laundry in a hospital must be carried out so as to prevent the dirty laundry from staying too long within the care departments, as this could be a potential vector for contamination and a possible source of a deterioration in the quality of the services overall (for example stains may become permanent). Further, the supply of clean linen from a hospital laundry can only come from the dirty laundry, which was sent in and which has been washed. The removal of dirty laundry and its return from the hospital laundry center are, therefore, two factors that govern how much clean linen can be produced and supplied to the services.

Similarly, for many other logistics flows, different containers that are used for providing supplies are also used for processing the supplies that are removed and for the subsequent flows. In the Troyes HC, for example, the same trolleys used to deliver the midday meal are also used to deliver the evening meal. Indeed, when opening their new logistics center (which contained a kitchen, laundry and central store) in 2009, the institution made the choice of investing in a single fleet of trolleys. Apart from the economic advantage (the savings in the purchasing costs of the trolleys), this also helped the hospital avoid the problem of finding a parking station for a second fleet of trolleys both in the care units as well as the logistics center itself, knowing that every additional square meter in a construction project adds on a non-negligible cost. However, while economically advantageous, this choice results in the need for very precise logistical planning: the Troyes HC meal trolleys must be brought to the logistics center as quickly as possible after the midday meal, so that they may be washed in the washing tunnel, complying with hygiene regulations, before being reused for the evening meal delivery.

Finally, waste represents a significant restriction, both in terms of a strict deadline as well as in terms of the volume that must regularly be removed from the care services. Given their care objectives and given the equipment that is used, especially disposable/single-use material, hospitals produce vast amounts of waste. The annual hospital waste in France is estimated to be 700,000 tons. Care activities produce different kinds of waste: household waste, waste that could pose the risk of infection, biodegradable waste (food and other naturally decomposing products), radioactive waste, laboratory effluents, chemical waste, cartons, electronic waste, etc. Strict regulations govern the removal of waste from care services and this removal must be carried out within a precise time frame. Waste produced from activities involving the risk of infection, household waste, and biodegradable waste must not remain in the care unit for more than 1 day. The major challenge of hospital logistics is, therefore, to organize waste collection at least once a day, including Saturdays, Sundays and other holidays. In the Troyes HC, waste collection is organized several times a day for each unit.

Hospital logistics flows are, thus, a continuous sequence of precisely timed requirements, both in terms of supplying departments as well as removing materials from departments. These demands may be more or less strenuous depending on the geographical restrictions (on-site production or production in a site distant from the hospital), architectural restrictions (the perimeter of the departments that must be supplied with material, the number of available freight elevators and so on) and the organizational choices the institution makes.

4.3.2. *The need for flexibility and reactivity*

Ensuring continuity in supplies to care departments depends, obviously, on ensuring adequate stocks in the care services. However, it may be that some supplies cannot be stored within the care departments. This is especially the case with medication that may be prescribed in an emergency situation. Thus, while deliveries of medicines to the care departments are planned twice a week at the Troyes HC, the pharmacy may need to urgently supply medicines to these departments, especially if a new patient is admitted or an existing patient requires a different course of treatment following changes in their state of health. Given the scope for these urgent and unforeseeable requirements, logistics deliveries in hospitals must be flexible and reactive. The organization of supplies to care services must, thus, respond to this paradoxical double requirement of regularity as well as flexibility.

4.3.3. *Qualitative requirements in supply and removal chains*

The supply and removal flows require that certain rules of hygiene be respected. Generally speaking, the flows to deliver meals, clean linen or sterile medical equipment, and the reverse flows, i.e. the removal of dirty linen, remains of meals and dirty crockery and *a fortiori* wastes, must be planned so as to avoid any mixing and any risk of contamination.

4.4. Challenges around the role played in enhancing the appeal of the institution

The smooth operations of logistics functions plays a role in the quality of care administered to patients and residents and, in this way, it contributes to the positive perception, and thus, the attractiveness of the institution. This aspect has become all the more important since the implementation of invoicing on a price-per-activity basis. Indeed, observing schedules for meal services and respecting good practices in meal delivery naturally contribute to the quality of the catering service and patient satisfaction. The regularity of laundry deliveries contributes to the comfort of patient care.

4.5. Challenges surrounding economic optimization

In the context of the financing of hospital activity through the pricing-per-activity, based on invoices that are largely paid through medical insurance, hospital logistics cannot escape the need for economic optimization. This requirement is all the more significant given that the logistics functions of the hospital, the support functions for care services, do not themselves bring any revenue to the hospital.

Hospital functions thus face the challenge of sending supplies to and removing material from care departments within the given schedule and at a given frequency, ensuring a continuity in supplies – all at lowest possible cost. The cost of logistics functions is naturally evaluated as a comprehensive cost, i.e. by simultaneously calculating the cost of materials, maintenance, having a dedicated logistics structure and the cost of the personnel put in charge of these functions.

For transport services within the institutions, economic performance is evaluated based on the number of employees assigned to the transport functions, the cost of the required vehicles, the distances to cover to carry out logistical deliveries (which translates into a fuel-consumption cost and a greater or smaller cost of wear-and-tear on the vehicles). This is why, in 2015, the Champagne Sud hospitals launched a study on the optimization of logistics flows focusing on transport, which resulted, in 2016, in concrete improvements in the organization of the Aube public mental health facility (EPSMA – établissement de santé mentale de l'Aube) and the Troyes HC.

4.5.1. *Examples of optimization implementations*

In the EPSMA, a team of drivers carried out deliveries of laundry, meals, pharmaceutical products, supplies to the central store as well the removal of dirty laundry, serving all buildings in the Brienne-le-Château hospital and also all the main sites in the EPSMA, located primarily at Troyes and Romilly-sur-Seine. These deliveries used to be carried out by a team of drivers, two of whom also worked as automobile mechanics in the EPSMA garage[7].

---

7 The EPSMA has its own auto-repair garage to care for their vehicles, as they have a fleet of 80 vehicles, which are used for the activities of the various annexes of the institution over

The delivery of meals comprised a large part of the responsibilities of these teams: the meals produced in the kitchens of the Troyes HC, located at Saint-Julien-les-Villas, were, initially, picked up from Saint-Julien six days a week and would then be stored in refrigerators in the former central kitchen of the Brienne-Le-Château hospital. The meals would then be delivered all seven days a week, before the mealtimes, to each care department within the EPSMA, located in different buildings within the institution. The installation of refrigerators in the care departments made it possible to directly deliver meals to each care department, thus avoiding the break in the cold chain resulting from the time-consuming task of unloading and storing the food in the former central kitchen. Further, one set of drivers from the Troyes HC would carry out the delivery of meals within the Troyes site of the EPSMA, while another team of drivers carried out deliveries to an institution located in the same street. It was, therefore, more efficient to have these meals also delivered by the Troyes HC drivers.

This new organization of deliveries resulted in 2.5 h being saved each day. This made it possible for the team of drivers to carry away waste from the care services as well as allowing for a new job post to be created in the team. The task of carrying away of wastes was, in fact, earlier carried out by the gardening team of the institution, which was stretched for time and once the task was redistributed to the drivers, the gardening team was able to refocus their energies on maintaining the park around the Brienne castle. This also illustrates the advantage of putting in place a joint organization of logistics deliveries to two institutions.

Today the same scope for optimization exist between various establishments: deliveries of pharmaceutical supplies and non-pharmaceutical supplies are carried out across all the sites of the EPSMA located close to other Champgne Sud hospital facilities, especially in Romilly-sur-Seine, Bar-sur-Seine and Bar-sur-Aube.

With respect to the Troyes HC, the teams from internal departments in the hospital carry out the deliveries of meals, laundry, supplies from the central store and pharmacy supplies in heavy logistics vehicles and 3.5T vehicles. These flows are carried out not only between the logistics center for the

all territories in the region, and for activities outside the hospital (psychiatric services in the region).

facility located at Saint-Julien-les-Villas and the different hospital sites located in the Troy agglomeration (the Hauts Clos hospital, the Comte Henri residence and the Nazareth estate) but are also directed toward its partner establishments (the Bar-sur-Seine hospital centers, the Aube public mental health facility located at Brienne-le-Château, the Pasteur functional re-education and re-adaptation center located at Troye, and the Méry-sur-Seine, Arcis-sur-Aube, Chaource and Riceys retirement homes) whose meals and linen are supplied by the kitchen and laundry from the same facility. The flows also move from the Simone Veil hospital pharmacy toward the institution's other sites (the Comte Henri residence and the Nazareth estate).

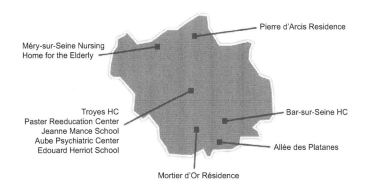

Figure 4.5. *Delivery carried out by the department within the Troyes HC at the beginning of the logistics optimization process that was undertaken in 2016*

When the optimization study began, the department within the Troyes HC carried out the deliveries with a fleet of five vehicles and five drivers from Monday to Friday, three drivers on Saturday and two drivers on Sunday. The vehicles used for the deliveries were hired on contract for an annual cost of 89,215 euros per year in 2015. The drivers were a team of 12. The fuel costs were estimated to be 22,000 euros per year. The aim of this study was to optimize the drivers' time as well as the number of vehicles used and the distance traveled.

The project that used mathematical optimization of the flows finally made it possible, in 2016, to carry out the same supply flows with four drivers from Monday to Friday and only two drivers on Saturday. This optimization was based on a review of the principles underlying the organization of the transport until then. These were, namely:

– assigning a near-exclusive vehicle for each type of flow: thus, of the five vehicles used, two were exclusively assigned for the transport of meals, one was exclusively assigned for the transport of linen, one was exclusively assigned for deliveries of supplies to the central store and the last vehicle – a 3.5T vehicle – was also used for delivering linen to partner establishments that were difficult to access as well as for pharmaceutical deliveries. This contributed, notably, to the vehicle traveling empty several times, when returning from a supply or removal run, as well as time spent waiting with an empty vehicle at the logistics center (amounting to 1,524 h a year, roughly the equivalent of a full-time driver for the year)[8];

– assigning one driver per vehicle: each driver drove the same vehicle all through the day. This was a major factor contributing to the rigidity of the system and the increase in demand for drivers.

On the condition that the systematic use of the refrigerated vehicles would continue for the delivery of meals, the flows were planned in such a way as to minimize the demands on drivers, vehicles and the distances covered.

This new form of organization has resulted in a saving of at least one job post across the team of 12, representing an economic gain of 30,000 €. The annual waiting time of the drivers between two journeys was reduced from 1,524 to 432 h. This optimization would also have made it possible to remove a vehicle from the fleet of five, but the institution was constrained to keep five vehicles for practical reasons: the access path to one of the partner establishments was so narrow that no vehicle larger than a 3.5T truck could serve this site. The success of these optimization measures at the Troyes HC and the EPSMA illustrates the potential for improvement in existing logistics functions within the Champagne Sud hospitals. The optimization process

---

8 It must be noted that the "dirty" flows (used laundry, returning used meal trays, etc.) must be set apart from clean flows (delivering clean laundry, delivering meals, etc.), i.e. these flows must be transported in different vehicles unless the vehicle is disinfected between deliveries, as is now done for the flows transported by the internal department in the Troyes HC since the logistics center opened in 2019. This made it possible to use the same vehicles for both the fresh supplies as well as used supplies. The logistics vehicles are disinfected after each journey at the logistics center.

carried out in the Troyes HC also demonstrated the need to optimize logistics flow management tools in order for efficient economic optimization.

4.5.2. *Challenges in optimizing logistics flow management tools*

Moving from five drivers to four, for the deliveries carried out by the Troyes HC, as well as the rethinking of the practices of assigning a single driver to the same vehicle for an entire day and of using one vehicle for each type of flow, all represented major changes in the job description of the drivers. Their work hours were significantly modified, although the institution committed to maintaining the average weekly working hours as before (37.5 h per week). The transformation of the optimized working hours, in the rough form produced by the simulations, into working hours that would be compatible with regulations relating to work timings in the world of public hospitals (limited to a maximum of 10.5 h, mandatory breaks after 6 h of work, mandatory periods of at least 3 h in the case of non-continuous works, i.e. work with a meal-time break of at least 30 min in the course of the day, etc.) as well as with European regulations regarding the driving of heavy vehicles (limited to a driving time of 4.5 h at a stretch) was an extremely time-consuming task.

It was also necessary that drivers could refer to daily task sheets that described the sequences of tasks to be carried out and the vehicles to be used and reminded them of the time constraints in place. The optimization process thus revealed that it was essential to implement a software that would make it possibly to quickly carry out not only simulations for how best to organize the drivers' working hours, but also simulations for working hours for the workstations that were involved, respecting regulations, as well as the daily task sheets and the loading of different trolleys into the trucks.

The Champagne Sud hospitals thus developed an optimization software for the logistics distribution rounds, responding to this need. This software was developed in conjunction with a specialized start-up, OTPA-LP, a logistics optimization consultancy associated with the University of Technology of Troyes. The specific development of this software illustrates the distance that must still be traveled in hospital logistics. Indeed, while the logistics sector has, for many years now, invested in the field of software to organize or optimize logistics, as with courier services and/or logistics transport, many hospital facilities, and especially the Champagne Sud hospitals, stayed away from this dynamic, creating a significant mismatch between their practices and the challenges, both qualitative as well as economic, for their transport functions. The Champagne Sud hospitals did, indeed, continue to follow a system of organization that was built up with a lot of good intentions and good sense, but devoid of any tool that would guarantee optimization, taking into account all the parameters to be considered. The immediate future of the performance of hospital logistics functions will, undoubtedly, involve the automation of tools to aid in the optimization of logistics flows, extending to scheduling and to the daily task sheets for drivers. Tools of this type are also essential to support the regional dimension that any hospital logistics optimization program will consider.

4.6. Challenges related to regional cooperation

The logistics sector is one of the fields within which public health facilities have established long-standing cooperative practices (Fédération Hospitalière de France 2011). There are, thus, several cooperative measures, dating back several years, around laundry, meal distribution, pharmaceutical and central store supplies as well as sterilization functions. The present economic context, with shrinking resources, within which many health establishments and territorialization practices operate, naturally reinforces the dynamic of regional cooperation around logistics functions.

4.6.1. *Cooperative purchasing in the context of regional hospital consortia*

Law 2016-41, dated January 26, 2016, on the modernization of France's health system, made it mandatory for public health facilities in the same region to coordinate around a common and graduated strategy for administering care to patients in the context of a regional hospital consortium (RHC). This involves, in particular, developing a shared medical project, setting up affiliated regional care centers and organizing a calibrated care offer in order to guarantee equal access to safe and high-quality healthcare. Within the framework of this law, the RHC will guarantee the rationalization of management practices through a pooling of functions or transferring certain activities from one establishment to another.

Consequently, from July 2016 onward, all public health institutions in France were grouped into 135 regional health consortia, with each RHC developing around a support institution which was responsible for overseeing organizing functions and delegated activities for the other member institutions. In order for institutions belonging to an RHC to be able to develop and implement their shared medical goals, this law provided for a set of tools or practices that had to be shared by all institutions. Notable among these was the case of purchases (Article 1 2016). The law also made provisions for setting up a common organization for biological, imaging and pharmaceutical services. Finally, the law envisaged the possibility of members of an RHC pooling their logistics functions.

In concrete terms, from January 1, 2018 onward the support institution in an RHC was put in charge of purchasing functions on behalf of all the member institutions of that RHC. This means that this institution is also assigned the responsibility of developing policies, schedules and strategies for all contracts for the RHC and also awarding or procuring these contracts (Article 2 2017). This joint purchasing in the context of an RHC is part of a larger movement to pool hospital purchases, which has grown exponentially since the mid-2000s. Hospital purchases have now been pooled with the creation of nationwide purchase agreements (such as UNIHA or RESAH, which are networks for purchases for the hospital), in addition to using UGAP, a central public purchasing service and regional purchase groups, which have chiefly developed within the context of project PHARE (the national plan for carrying out hospital purchases).

As a result of the creation of grouped markets and the implementation of the RHCs, purchases are increasingly being made on a shared basis by regional hospital consortia. Further, in the pharmaceutical products market, which is the primary area of spending for purchasing products to be used within the institutions[9], the development of RHCs further strengthens the territorial structure of pharmacies, which was already in place in certain regions.

---

9 Medication and medical devices represent, on the national level, purchases of 4.6 billion euros and 3.5 billion euros, respectively, from a total amount of 18 billion euros spent on hospital purchases.

While the execution of contracts as well as supplies, i.e. managing orders to suppliers to whom a particular contract is awarded (as well as the processing of the corresponding invoices), is not transferred to the support institution by law, it is clear that the pooling of purchases in an RHC and the dynamic of a territorial structure for pharmaceutical operations introduce a tendency to carry out cooperative actions around supplies and storage.

The strategy of creating one or more common storage centers between the institutions of an RHC deserves to be considered in greater detail.

In these conditions, as concerns the institutions that form the RHC of Aube and Sézannais, whose members include several institutions of the Champagne Sud hospitals as well as other medico-social and privative partner institutes in the regions, the chief concern is to reflect on a strategy for maximum pooling of logistics functions.

4.6.2. *Challenges around common supplies and storage*

The logistics sector in Europe, and especially in France, is structured around regional concentrations of businesses and the installation of a logistics center in a region situated so as to be in proximity to the centers of consumption in order to reduce costs. Distribution chains between suppliers and public health institutions are also governed by this organizational plan. Further, for better performance, the public contracts awarded by the hospital purchasing groups increasingly tend toward supplies being delivered in massive quantities to hospitals[10] on the assumption that prices will be lower for a bulk order. The pooling of deliveries does, naturally, result in lower logistics costs, which are then reflected in the suppliers quoting lower prices in the public contract.

With the sharing of contracts between institutions in an RHC, the other members of the group will gradually purchase the same reference products from the same suppliers. The positive economic impact of this growing volume of purchases may be reinforced by creating common deliveries to all members of the RHC. This presupposes common storage facilities for these

---

10 As is the case, for example, with products that protect against incontinence, hand-sanitizer supplies, etc.

institutions. Developing a strategy along these lines would provide opportunities for optimization for the member institutions in the Aube and Sézannais RHC.

4.6.2.1. *Challenges surrounding the pooling of central store supplies between institutions*

The pooling of deliveries and stores for several institutions in the RHC will make it possible to re-internalize the functions currently carried out by private logistics companies (storage, transport). For the institutions in the Aube and Sézannais RHC, the basic design would be that of organizing three warehouses in the three principal institutions in such a way as to cover the entire region, both for the institutions in the RHC as well as their partner institutions. This pooling of stores will also enable the sharing of warehouse management tools. At present, only the support institution uses a Warehouse Management System (WMS), which is a software for managing stocks, suggesting what orders to place and the optimization of stores within a warehouse. Of course, this is only a viable measure if these institutions are able to carry out this re-internalization of functions at a lower overall cost than the amount charged by the logistics companies.

Thus, the prerequisites for this potential pooling of supplies and storage, and the creation of a regional structure for pharmaceutical services, are:

– the capacity to organize logistic flows between institutions in an efficient manner;

– upstream, the ability to rapidly simulate these flows so as to validate various hypotheses from studies on the regional structuring of the warehouses.

As concerns the ability to efficiently organize flows in the Champagne Sud hospitals, flows of logistics transport between the different institutions are already in place, resulting from existing cooperative practices around logistics. We can, therefore, envisage combining future flows of deliveries of supplies between the institutions with these existing flows, which could potentially result in flows that are more cost effective than the current distribution patterns used by private logistics companies.

With regard to the ability to rapidly simulate flows to verify performance, Champagne Sud hospitals saw the benefits of having a software that could carry this out and, thus, in conjunction with the company OPTA-LP, they developed a software module that made it possible to carry out these simulations and propose the optimal transport solutions. It is very possible that we will eventually arrive at a tool that can optimize not only the transport logistics using vehicles between the production sites (laundries, central kitchens, pharmacies, sterilizing units) and the different institutions but also internal transport logistics within larger institutions, at least for the Troyes HC. This would be a tool that would make it possible to optimize both transport in heavy goods vehicles as well as the handling of heavy automated guided vehicles (AGV).

Map of members of the
Aube and Sézannais
RHC

Figure 4.6. *A map showing members of the Aube and Sézannais RHC. For a color version of this figure, see www.iste.co.uk/blua/hospital.zip*

Apart from the need to be able to simulate and organize logistical flows between institutions, creating common stores first requires standardizing the products consumed by each institution. This work can, obviously, be facilitated by the pooling of public contracts, as provided by the RHC. However, this joint purchasing must be accompanied by a rigorous evaluation of the consumption of each type of product in each establishment. This assumes, first of all, that it is possible to inventory all the reference products bought by each establishment in a harmonized manner. At present, the same code could refer to two different products in two different Champagne Sud institutions. Conversely, the same product may be referred to by two different names in two different institutions.

The convergence of information systems, which must be implemented by 2020 as per the RHC regulations, will make it possible to manage purchases and outgoing stock for establishments using an identical software based on nomenclature that will be common to all the institutions, thereby facilitating the pooling of stores between the institutions that are part of the Champagne Sud hospitals.

4.6.2.2. *Challenges surrounding joint placing of orders and invoice processing*

At present, each institution places its own orders with their suppliers to buy stores of supplies. This, thus, results in there being as many orders placed as there are establishments. The pooling of stores and supplies between institutions does, of course, presuppose a single order being placed for all the institutions.

Indeed, it is impossible to consider pooling stocks and deliveries by suppliers without placing joint orders. It would be counterproductive for each establishment to continue placing their own orders, causing a fivefold increase in the workload. However, inasmuch as each institution retains its own legal personality, how can we legally put in place a common order for five establishments? At present, the laws relating to the RHC provide for the transfer of the procurement competence to the support institution, that is to the Troyes HC. However, the legislation does not provide for transferring, to this institution, the power to supply to nor the possibility of placing orders on behalf of the other institutions.

In these conditions, a possible solution would be the creation of a Healthcare Cooperation Consortium (HCC)[11], endowed with a moral

---

11 A healthcare cooperation consortium is a form of cooperation that is endowed with a moral personality. The HCC for resources aim to develop the activities of their member establishments

personality, making it possible to carry out joint orders for all supplies stocked within the establishments of the Champagne Sud hospitals.

Despite the advantages, the creation of such a structure also represents a heavy workload for management: deadlines for approval for the creation of this structure from the regional health authorities, the nomination of an accountant for the structure, choosing whether it should be a public enterprise or a private enterprise depending on the composition of the structure, management of specialized accounting for purchasing supplies and re-invoicing the institutions who benefit from the service.

It is possible, however, to avoid the onerous task of setting up a new structure by using an existing cooperative structure: the PIG[12] for interhospital logistics in Aube. This is a legal structure that covers cooperation around laundry and refreshment functions. It is also possible to envisage the creation of an HCC in the future for managing pharmaceutical functions within the hospitals (see section 4.6.3). Similarly, it is possible to envisage that the support institution may become the buyer for other institutions; however this would require a significant adaptation of legislative texts.

In the meanwhile, it is already possible to envisage the pooling of orders for supplies for these institutions, i.e. the creation of a centralized team who will place orders as well as carry out the processing of invoices. This joint ordering and invoicing can also be put in place without waiting for the pooling of stocks. This would have the advantage of facilitating the creation of a homogeneous nomenclature across establishments to refer to products. This homogeneity would result from shared databases to record these products and through the same group of people processing the orders for these products for all the establishments.

---

and, to this end, they may organize or manage administrative, logistical, technical, medico-technical, pedagogic or research activities; they may establish or manage teams with common goals and allow medical and non-medical professionals from their member establishments, as well as independent consultants who are affiliated to the consortium, to work within any member institution. The healthcare institutions within the HCC may hold a license for healthcare activities.

12 PIGs or public interest groups are cooperative structures developed under public law, endowed with a moral personality comprising several moral persons who pool together their resources in order to carry out not-for-profit activities for public benefit.

4.6.3. *Challenges surrounding the pooling of pharmaceutical supplies*

The pooling of pharmaceutical supplies represents a particular challenge, within the overall challenges surrounding the pooling of supplies. Each of the five institutions within the Champagne Sud hospitals today has an internal-use pharmacy (IUP), i.e. an in-house pharmacy that carries out the preparation and dispensing of medication[13] and other pharmaceutical products to the care services.

The major challenges related to the dispensing of pharmaceutical products are related to reinforcing the safety of dispensing drugs by implementing an automated nominative dispensing software for medicine in all establishments under the Champagne Sud hospitals. Nominative dispensation refers to a system of organization where medicines are prepared by the pharmacy and delivered to care departments in single doses for each patient[14]. Automation assumes the availability of automatons that will carry out this nominative dispensation. In fact, results from French studies converge to indicate a significant contribution by nominative dispensation in adding to safety in medicinal care. Daily dispensation is the frequency recommended in the medicine, surgery and obstetrics (MSO) departments.

Further, the automation of dispensation will considerably reduce the risk of human error in the preparation of a prescription. At present, not all establishments under the Champagne Sud hospitals, have the automated nominative dispensation facility available: most dispensing of drugs is still carried out manually in all the establishments[15]. Furthermore, for a number of MSO services the dispensing is still carried out on a weekly basis. For some residential institutions for the elderly run by this hospital, dispensation occurs on a monthly basis.

---

13 The dispensing of medication is defined according to the terms of the order dated April 6, 2011 concerning the quality of medicinal care and medicines within the healthcare institutions, as well as according to the Pharmaceutical Act that covers the delivery and pharmaceutical analysis of medical prescriptions, the preparation of doses to administer (if needed) and the making available of information and advice on the appropriate use of medication.

14 Nominative dispensation may be carried out on variable schedules (daily, weekly, monthly).

15 Apart from the long-term residential facility and senior citizen home in the Nazareth estate and the Comte Henri residence in the Troyes hospital center, which have already installed automated dispensing services.

The objective for the Champagne Sud hospitals is, therefore, to put in place a daily nominative dispensing system for MSO, a bi-weekly system for post-acute care and rehabilitation services, and a weekly system for retirement homes. To respond to the demands made by the nominative dispensing system, the institutions must be able to prepare the prescription in unit doses or carry out overpackaging that makes it possible to individualize the doses and identify the medicine all along its circuit, until it is finally administered to the patient.

Given that a large portion of medication is still not delivered in single dose packaging in hospital facilities in France, the first step toward this would be to organize the relabeling or overpackaging of medication. This step may be extremely time consuming and could also result in a considerable risk of error if carried out manually. The safety of this first step, therefore, is also ensured by the automation of the process.

In the context of this goal of ensuring the safety and automation of the dispensing of medicines, the HSC put in place the goal of creating a common regional organization for their pharmacies. This new regional organization will, first of all, be based on the centralizing of all pharmaceutical deliveries and the automated unpackaging or overpackaging carried out in the Troyes HC (the support institution); it will also be based on implementing the automated preparation of deliveries in three establishments, that is, the installation of automatons for dispensing medication in three establishments under the Champagne Sud hospitals (in the Troyes HC, the Romilly-sur-Seine hospital and the Aube public mental health facility).

The regional structuring of the pharmacy assumes that there has been detailed planning around the flow of medicines and other pharmaceutical products between the establishments that come under the Champagne Sud hospitals.

The efficiency of such a system will depend on the effectiveness of the transport system, both in terms of finding the most economically advantageous solution as well as in terms of organizing fresh supplies on an urgent basis (for example if there are new patients admitted or emergency changes in treatment).

Apart from the implementation of a software architecture allowing for the interfacing of the institution's economic and financial management systems with the electronic patient records software for each establishment, the pharmaceutical validation of prescriptions, and the transversal management of pharmaceutical stocks across the different institutions involved, this new organization will also require the use of a tool to optimize the logistics flows discussed in section 4.5.2.

4.6.4. *Challenges around pooling fleets of vehicles*

The different establishments that come under the Champagne Sud hospitals all possess a fleet of service vehicles, commercial vehicles and, for the large part, light vehicles. These vehicles are used for the different tasks carried out by hospital agents that require them to travel (a meeting on another site or establishment, advanced consultations, etc.). These vehicles are either available to all hospital employees, upon reservation, for a given task or are directly allocated to a department (for instance for activities related to hospitalization at home (hospitalisation à domicile, HAD) or for the activities of the home nursing services (Service de soins infirmiers à domicile, SSIAD) of the Aube Marne hospital consortia, for activities carried out outside the Aube public mental health facility[16] and for mobile palliative care units).

The combined fleet of vehicles across the five establishments that make up the Champagne Sud hospitals is particularly large, with 178 light vehicles[17] (cars as well as commercial vehicles). There are, similarly, 59 vehicles in the

---

16 Psychiatric care outside the hospital is defined as care administered outside a complete hospitalization structure. This refers to care provided in MPCs (medico-psychological centers: consultation sites that offer ambulatory care, preventive action and also follow-ups at home), PTTCs (part-time therapy centers: centers that offer care that aims to maintain or promote the autonomy of patients through support actions and group therapy), day clinics, *accueil familial thérapeutique* or therapeutic foster care (a system where adults or children who require care are taken in by a foster family), post-cure centers, etc. This type of care-giving occupies an important place in psychiatric treatments. Indeed, a circular dated March 15, 1960, fixed the goal of promoting the reintegration of patients into society by promoting the resolution of their medico-social problems through the division of regions into sectors. Each sector would have a medical and paramedical team who would administer care to patients at all stages of an illness, from the initial medical screening to reintegration into society; hospitalization was just another step in the treatment of the illness. Non-hospital psychiatric activities have a high requirement for vehicles, especially for home visits, care provided at home and follow-up visits for therapy in foster families.
17 Numbers collected in 2015.

Aube Marne hospital consortium since the institution is organized across three sites and due to the HAD and SSIAD activities carried out (22 vehicles). The public mental health facility has 75 light vehicles[18], chiefly due to the activities carried out outside the hospital across the entire region, within the framework of the division of each region into sectors[19], which requires 24 vehicles.

The challenges around the management of the fleet reside in meeting the requirement of optimizing management costs, which involves, in particular, reducing the size of the fleet, while continuing to satisfy user needs. Indeed, setting up the common directorate for the Champagne Sud hospitals and for the RHC, as well as the development of advanced consultations, has resulted in a significant increase in the movement of employees. Cutting down on the number of vehicles will, then, result in lower rates of obsolescence across the fleet by focusing means on the most necessary vehicles. The costs are, indeed, quite high, in terms of operational costs (for example, the hiring charges as well as the maintenance costs for the vehicles). Thus, the challenges for the Champagne Sud hospitals are:

– pooling the fleet of vehicles in such a way that the maximum number of vehicles are at the disposal of all departments of an institution, instead of being allocated to a single department;

– carry out this pooling of fleets at a regional level.

Indeed, the sites of the satellite units of the EPSMA in the sector have coincided, in many cases, with the sites of the other establishments of the Champagne Sud hospitals: the satellite centers of the EPSMA in Bar-sur-Aube and Bar-sur-Seine (for children) are, respectively, located on the sites of the Bar-sur-Aube and Bar-sur-Seine hospital centers. It would, therefore, be possible to think of the hospital center fleet being shared with the EPSMA teams.

Moreover, as concerns the pooling of services, a study carried out in the Troyes HC in 2016 showed, for example, that of the two vehicles allocated to the palliative care unit, both vehicles were in use only once every 4 days and all

---

18 Figures from 2016.

19 Psychiatric care was organized on a sector-wise basis since the publication of the circular of March 15, 1960 mentioned above. The region is divided into different sectors and the medical and paramedical team in each sector administer both hospital and non-hospital care.

other days a single vehicle sufficed for the unit's requirements. This example illustrates an obvious potential for pooling. Nonetheless, the difficulty resides in any immediate and unforeseen requirement for the vehicles that might come up, given that they are used by the palliative care units. This team may need to use a vehicle on a sudden, unplanned basis, for instance, to respond to an emergency assessment of the health of a patient who may potentially require palliative care at home. These demands, however, do not completely preclude the possibility of sharing resources: pooling remains possible with, perhaps, the systematic sharing of one of the vehicles used by the palliative care unit with other departments, based on a specific schedule, and by reserving the second vehicle on a priority basis for palliative care.

Figure 4.7. *A map showing the sectors and non-hospital adult psychiatric care centers operated by the EPSMA. For a color version of this figure, see www.iste.co.uk/blua/hospital.zip*

The pooling of vehicles between services and institutions requires a high-performing reservation software for managing and following up on the use of these vehicles. Very precise information must be filled in when placing a request for these vehicles and this information will allow the software to automatically collect statistics on the use of the vehicles, which will then serve as a database to optimize the fleet, keeping in mind the actual demands made on the vehicles: optimizing the size of the vehicles used depending on the number of passengers, optimizing the choice of diesel engines versus petrol engines depending on the actual distances covered and average distance traveled, etc. We can consider the possibility of combining this software with a geolocalization system in the vehicles, allowing for an automatic calculation of the distances covered and the use of the vehicles.

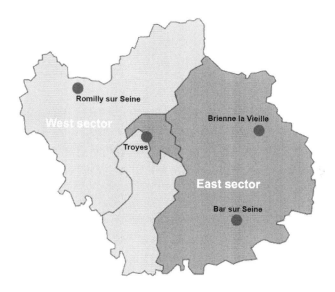

Figure 4.8. *A map showing the sectors and non-hospital psychiatric care centers for children and adolescents operated by the EPSMA. For a color version of this figure, see www.iste.co.uk/blua/hospital.zip*

At present, the modalities for reserving the vehicles and the data on vehicle use are only noted manually. Consequently, carrying out statistical calculations becomes a very complicated task. Here again, the challenges surrounding optimization are combined with the challenges of computerizing and digitizing of tools.

4.7. Challenges surrounding the implementation of a regional supply chain management

A supply chain refers to the logistical chain involved in moving supplies from source to destination. The concept of *supply chain management* refers to the coordination of all resources, means, methods, tools and techniques that are used to move the supplies with the greatest efficiency possible from the first supplier to the final client. This is, therefore, a transversal approach that requires a good coordination across all the steps in the logistics chain. For hospitals, this may involve working with suppliers to work on solutions that involve direct deliveries to the concerned departments or pre-packaging (an upstream process whereby the supplier groups the supplies into parcels based on the recipient within the hospital services). Supply chain management also aims to position the logistics chain as supplier of services vis-à-vis care services.

In this context, the challenges for the institutions that come under the Champagne Sud hospitals or the Aube and Sézannais RHC consist of applying supply chain management to the new regional organization that consists of pooling logistics and logistical processes across institutions, with the supply chain extending from the suppliers up to the final care units that will take charge of the supplies. In this framework, the digital challenge is that of making available common software tools that can efficiently optimize the entire logistics chain across institutions: WMSs (refer to section 4.6.2.1) for the management of stores, a tool for the combined implementation of flows between institutions and the flows within institutions and also tools used for e-procurement (i.e. tools whereby care services can directly place orders with suppliers for supplies that are not stored) and a virtual supply portal (to manage orders).

The logistics functions carried out throughout hospitals (managing orders, storage, transport functions, etc.) are the pivot of this supply chain. The recent implementation of a transversal Directorate of Purchases and Logistics within the Champagne Sud hospitals (which could also potentially serve other partner institutions in the RHC) could be the opportunity needed to create, over the next few years, a true logistics support function based on supply chain management, which would no longer simply be the juxtaposition of logistics functions of each institutions but would be transformed into a true integrated, transversal department, playing a crucial role in driving the supply chain.

4.8. Conclusion

The principal challenges surrounding logistics in the Champagne Sud hospitals are therefore (going beyond the need to ensure safety and continuity in supplies):

– the optimization of logistics performance by the professionalization and systematization of scientific research into the most cost-effective solutions using software tools that must be implemented both for the organization of logistics flows between establishments as well as the management of automobile fleets, as carried out in sectors apart from the hospital sector;

– implementing, high-performing regional organization (using these optimization measures) of pharmaceutical functions, supplies, storage and cooperation around logistics in the context of the Aube and Sézannais RHC.

It is essential that hospital logistics is able to respond to the needs of the care service activities and be efficient. This is dependent on technological measures, namely the implementation of digital tools, based on mathematical tools, to process the entirety of the supply chain for these organizations.

4.9. References

Décret no. 2017-701 relatif aux modalités de mise en oeuvre des activités, fonctions et missions (2017). Article L6132-3 du code de la santé publique, au sein des groupements hospitaliers de territoire [Online]. Available: https://www.legifrance.gouv.fr/affichTexte.do?cidTexte=JORFTEXT 000034566831&categorieLien=id.

Fédération Hospitalière de France. (2011). Recensement des coopérations et des projets de coopération association des établissements publics de santé, sociaux et médico-sociaux quel que soit leur statut juridique [Online]. Available: http://www.fhf.fr/Offre-de-soins-Qualite/Cooperation-entre-etablis-sements-et-reseaux/Diffusion-d-un-recensement-et-d-une-boite-a-outils-des-cooperations/Recensement-des-cooperations.

Le Moigne, R. (2017). *Supply Chain Management*. Dunod, Paris.

Loi no. 2016-41 de modernisation de notre système de santé. (2016). Article L 6132-3 du code de la santé publique [Online]. Available: https://www.legifrance.gouv.fr/eli/loi/2016/1/26/AFSX1418355L/jo/article _107.

Opta IP. [Online]. Available: https://www.opta-lp.com [Accessed 20 December 2018].

Forecasting Patient Flows into Emergency Services

5.1. Introduction

In recent years, certain modern hospitals have been able to implement some remarkable developments in the range of care services they can offer their patients (Kutty 2000; Gilson 2003; Banerjee *et al.* 2004). Emergency services (ES) represent the chief gateway for patients into the hospital and particular attention has been paid to these services in the attempts to offer in-patients a higher quality of service. Indeed, over the past few decades, the ES have seen a significant increase in the inflow of patients (Boyle *et al.* 2012; Yu *et al.* 2016). In numbers, the regional emergency observatory in Champagne Ardennes (a public organization that is meant to collect and analyze data from regional ES) stated that the number of visits to the ES in the Champagne Ardennes administrative territory increased by 6.43% per year from 2008 to 2013 (Panorama Urgences 2013). This phenomenon had a considerable impact on the management of ES in the region, especially in the Troyes hospital center (THC).

Several countries have studied the problem of the overcrowding of ES as well as the heavy consequences of this crowding (Derlet *et al.* 2001; Foley M. *et al.* 2011). Researchers have examined the causes and impact of this phenomenon (Sun *et al.* 2013; Yu *et al.* 2016) and have proposed various

Chapter written by Mohamed AFILAL, Lionel AMODEO, Farouk YALAOUI and Frédéric DUGARDIN.

solutions to improve the quality of services offered by the ES (Gendreau *et al.* 2007; Lin *et al.* 2008; Atallah and Lee 2010; Coskun and Erol 2010; Ajmi *et al.* 2013; Luo *et al.* 2016). Among the principal causes that these researchers put forth for the crowding of the ES, we have insufficient resources (human and material) (Cooke *et al.* 2004), an increase in the inflow of patients (Panorama Urgences 2013) and epidemics (Schull *et al.* 2005).

Several proposals have been discussed in available literature to solve this problem. We find, first of all, an inherent solution that aims to increase resources available to the ES in order to better absorb the increased inflow of patients through an expansion in the number of sites and/or the size of the staff. However, this kind of solution is less likely to be adapted by all health institutions (unless the city or town involved sees a critical demographic growth) due to the high costs resulting from the adoption of these policies. Further, in some cases, as cited by (Han *et al.* 2007), this type of action may be an inadequate solution for the improvement of the quality of service given to patients. An alternative that would guarantee an improvement in the quality of services in an ES, without requiring an increase in resources, is the optimization of resource allocation. We can refer here to work published by Gendreau *et al.* (2007), who explored the allocation of doctors in an ES. While human resources (doctors, nurses, etc.) are the principal resources in an ES, other research groups explored the optimization of all resources – human and material resources (Atallah and Lee 2008; Lin *et al.* 2008; Ajmi *et al.* 2013).

Before hastening toward solutions that aim to optimize the organization of a service, the decision-maker must certainly have some idea of what patient load they are looking at in the future. In other words, the forecasting of demand, represented in our case by the number of patients, is a crucial and primordial step that must be taken before the optimization of the organization. Several studies have been carried out in this context in order to predict patient flows in the hospital world, especially for the inflow of patients into the ES. Time series have proven to be a good tool to predict the levels of demand in different domains (de Gooijer and Hyndman 2006). The efficacy of this tool depends on the use of historic data for a particular phenomenon in order to establish a mathematical model that may be used to predict the behavior of this phenomenon in the future.

The main objective of this chapter is to build a model to predict the daily flow of patients both in the long term as well as in the short term. The goal of this predictive model is to predict the daily flow of patients for every category in the CCMU (the clinical classification of patients in ES) and the GEMSA (the multi-center study group of reception services) (Panorama Urgences 2013). In the step where we analyze data (a pre-requisite for constructing the model), we propose a new practical classification of patients in the ES, which groups together patients who exhibit similar behavior in the department.

5.2. The problem statement

The random nature of the arrival of patients in ES complicates the problem of managing this flow. Thus, forecasting the flow of patients will allow staff to manage their activities better. For more efficient management, the forecasting must take into account the pathology of the incoming patients. In fact, the ES receives different cases every day, requiring varied medical care that must be adapted to each case. This, in turn, requires a system of categorizing patients, where patient flow is predicted for each category.

Before beginning the analysis of patient flows to establish predictive models, we must define the time horizon and the periodicity of the predictions (hourly, daily, weekly, etc.). The ES of the THC currently manages its staff on a daily basis and, therefore, our objective was to predict how many patients come into the emergency services everyday. This approach will allow us to adapt the daily scheduling of personnel depending on the forecasting. Further, the teams are managed in 24-h time slots starting from 8 a.m. (which is when the shifts change; Figure 5.1) and, therefore, the flow to be predicted is the number of patients received between 8 a.m. on a given day and 8 a.m. on the following day. For long-term management purposes, the administrative staff in the ES will need annual predictions for their activities so that they can put in place appropriate schedules for staff that will also respect French and European norms and work laws. The challenge here is to predict the number of patients that arrive on a daily basis in the ES over a given year.

Long-term (annual) predictions will allow administrative staff in the ES to better manage their human resources (doctors, nurses, care assistants), especially managing holidays as well as managing their material resources (opening/closing of treatment cubicles, purchase of supplies/equipment, etc.).

In this context, our goal is to establish predictive models that are capable of predicting patient inflow over 1 year.

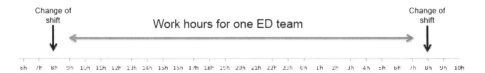

Figure 5.1. *The work hours for a team working in the ES*

Long-term predicting is an interesting tool for the strategic management of resources. However, it is limited in its usefulness in terms of adapting to changes in the behavior of patient flows coming into the services over the year. Indeed, the flow of patients in the ES may change from one year to the next depending on several factors such as the weather, the holiday season, epidemics and so on. Short-term prediction is an approach that makes it possible to predict a phenomenon in the near future (a few days ahead, in our case) by using a recent history of observations. Our goal, then, is to develop short-term predictive models that will enhance the accuracy of long-term models in order to remedy the problem of fluctuations in demand. This will allow staff to modify their scheduling in times of greater or lower patient flow.

An epidemic designates the rapid propagation of an illness that is generally contagious and infectious in origin, within a given population. The most likely epidemic-prone diseases in France today are seasonal flu, gastroenteritis and chickenpox. In each case, in order for an outbreak to be designated an epidemic, there is a pre-set threshold of cases per 100,000 residents (for instance, 80 cases per 100,000 residents for flu). These periods of epidemic have a significant impact on the number of patients visiting the ES. The majority of epidemics are of a seasonal nature, especially flu, which breaks out during winter. Nevertheless, these periods do not have a fixed duration or stable frequency from one year to another. Figure 5.2 shows the variation in the incidence rates of flu (number of cases per 100,000 residents) from 2010 to 2015. While we can clearly note the seasonal nature of the phenomenon (winter), it can also be seen that it does not start around the same date nor does it last for the same duration every year. Given the impact that these epidemics have on patient flows into the ES, it has been seen that the models must be robust and must include periods of epidemics as either exogenous or endogenous variables.

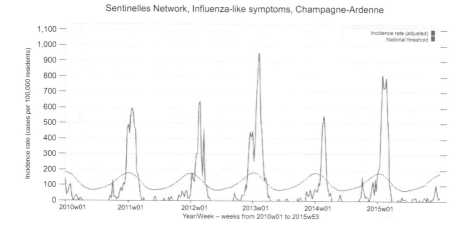

Figure 5.2. *A history of flu in the Champagne–Ardennes region from 2010 to 2015. For a color version of this figure, see www.iste.co.uk/blua/hospital.zip*

5.3. A state-of-the-art

The state-of-the-art is an essential step in any scientific project, as it makes it possible to analyze all existing research and to look for existing methods used to work on similar problems. We will, first of all, carry out a general analysis of existing predictive models in section 5.3.1 and then, in section 5.3.2, we will discuss the models applied for predicting the flow of patients into the ES.

5.3.1. *Predictive models*

Predicting demand has been the goal of scientific research since 1927, when Yule introduced a general approach to analyze and predict time series (Yule 1927). Following this work, there was considerable progress in the field of prediction with the appearance of the earliest methods of predicting time series, in the works of Yule, Slutsky and Walker (1931). They introduced the concept of autoregression (AR) and the moving average (MA) to predict a given phenomenon. These models were subsequently refined to become the ARMA (autoregressive – moving-average) model. This model was then improved and generalized using a methodology for analyzing and predicting time series, known as the Box and Jenkins method (Box and Jenkins 1971). However, in the case of seasonal phenomena, the basic ARMA/autoregressive integrated moving average (ARIMA) models are not efficient. Indeed, these are more appropriate for stationary phenomena and are incapable of following seasonal fluctuations. It was for this reason that the X-12-ARIMA extension was developed, specifically to work on the Findley and Monsell phenomena (Findley and Monsell 1998).

The importance and utility of prediction motivated researchers to develop several models to apply in different domains. After the ARMA models, the best-known models are based on exponential smoothing. These models came out of the work of (Brown 1959; Holt 2004) and (Winters 1960). This was known as the Holt–Winter model. We can also cite other types of models that have proven to be efficient in certain cases like artificial neuronal networks (ANN) (Aal 2008; Shahrabi *et al.* 2013; Crone *et al.* 2014), the support vector machine (SVM) models (Clarke *et al.* 2004; Hong 2009) and decision trees (Tso *et al.* 2007; Yang *et al.* 2008; Lam *et al.* 2010).

There is a vast scope of application for these tools. They give decision-makers an overview of the predicted activity in their services. Table 5.1 presents some examples for the use of prediction in different domains and over different time horizons. We can see that prediction is largely used in these different fields to predict the flow of demand.

Over the last three decades, researchers have studied the combining, mixing or hybridization of the different prediction methods. This approach consists of developing different models for the same phenomenon and bringing them together into a single model by weighing the values derived from each model by certain coefficients. Important contributions in this field have been made by Bates and Granger (1969); Newbold and Granger (1974) and Winkler and Makridakis (1983).

Convincing proof of the relative efficiency of combined forecasts, generally defined in terms of the variance of error in predicting, has been summarized by Clemen (1989) in a comprehensive bibliographic review. Many methods to select the combination weight have been proposed. The most widely used combination method is the simple average (Bunn 1985; Clemen 1989), but this method does not take into account earlier information on the precision of the forecasting nor the dependence between forecasts. Another, simpler approach is the linear summation of individual predictions, which combines the weights determined using the least square method (LSM) for the historical matrix of forecasts and observations (Granger and Ramanathan 1984). However, estimations resulting from the LSM are inefficient due to the possible presence of a serial correlation between the errors in the combined forecasts. Aksu and Gunter (1992) and Gunter (1992) have studied this problem in detail. They recommend the use of forecasts combined with LSM, with the weights being limited to unity. The combination of weights determined using methods that are invariable in time may lead to relatively weak forecasts if there is an absence of positioning between the forecasting of the components (Miller *et al.* 1992).

Data	Time horizons for prediction	Benchmarks	References
Prediction electricity	1–30 min	Wiener filter	(Di Caprio *et al.* 1983)
Quarterly automobile insurance paid	8 quarters	Log-linear regression	(Cummins and Griepentrog 1985)
Daily rate of federal funds	1 day	Random walk	(Hein and Spudeek 1988)
Macroeconomic quarterly data	1–8 quarters	Wharton model	(Dhrymes *et al.* 1988)
Monthly sales for large stores	1 month	Simple exponential smoothing	(Geurts and Kelly 1986)
Monthly demand for telephonic services	3 years	Univariate state space	(Grambsch and Stahel 1990)
Annual total of the population	20–30 years	Demographic models	(Pflaumer 1992)
Monthly touristic demand	1–24 months	Univariate state space, multivariate state space	(Du Preez and Witt 2003)
Monthly traffic of telecommunications	1 month	Univariate ARIMA	(Layton *et al.* 1986)
Daily call volume	1 week	Holt–Winters	(Bianchi *et al.* 1998)
Monthly sale of trucks	1–13 months	Univariate ARIMA, Holt–Winters	(Heuts and Bronckers 1988)
Monthly accounting data	1 month	Regression, univariate, ARIMA, transfer function	(Hillmer 1983)
Monthly movements of hospitalized patients	2 years	Univariate ARIMA, Holt–Winters	(Lin 1989)

Table 5.1. *Real-life examples of uses of prediction*

The shape of the combined distribution of the prediction error and the corresponding stochastic behavior was studied by De Menezes and Bunn (1998) and Taylor and Bunn (1999). For non-normal distributions of prediction error, evasion emerges as a relevant criterion for specifying the combination method. Fang (2003) has provided information on why competing forecasts may be successfully combined to produce a forecast that is superior to the individual forecasts, using the tests provided. Hibon and Evgeniou (2005) proposed a criterion to use to choose between forecasts and their combinations.

5.3.2. *Forecasting inflows into emergency services*

Forecasting the inflow patients into ES has been the aim of several research projects carried out in recent years. In 1988, Milner launched one of the first studies in this field, by developing the ARIMA forecasting models to forecast the total flow of patients in an ES (Milner 1988). These models, based on ARMA/ARIMA, have proven to be very effective and have been used in several research projects (Jones *et al.* 2002; Sun *et al.* 2009; Shi *et al.* 2011; Kadri *et al.* 2014).

The ARMA models are certainly the most widely studied and widely used models in this field. However, several researchers have also used other forecasting tools that have proven to be more appropriate for their specific research context, using linear or nonlinear models. In the linear model category, we can cite models based on linear regression (Ekström *et al.* 2014), multiple regression models (Boyle *et al.* 2008) and models based on exponential smoothing (Bergs *et al.* 2014). In the category of nonlinear models, we can cite the work done by Stout and Tawney (2005), who used an approach based on waiting lines to predict flows into emergency rooms, and work carried out by Mielczarek (2013), who used a Monte Carlo simulation approach. Specific approaches were used to predict the onset of a period of heavy demand (and not the number of patients, as in the classic cases). The best example of this is the work carried out by Bouleux *et al.* (2014), which offered a model that was capable of predicting the onset of a period of overpopulation in the Paediatrics Emergency Unit in Lille.

The exponential smoothing models have also been used in forecasting studies in hospitals (Hyndman *et al.* 2002; Medina *et al.* 2007). In the study carried out by Champion *et al.* (2007), the authors used the decomposition method to identify trends, seasons variations and the likelihood of "noise", to forecast the flows of patients in an ES. The authors then compared these forecasts, based on a simple seasonal exponential smoothing model, with an ARIMA model. Similarly, the study carried out by Medina *et al.* (2007) also identified seasonal oscillations and trends in the time series data on the phenomenon being studied.

The most recent research projects that are directly interested in forecasting patient flows in ES have been introduced by Aboagye Sarfo *et al.* (2015). The authors develop a multivariate vector ARMA model (VARMA) to forecast flows in an ES in Western Australia. A recent study carried out by Jalalpour *et al.* (2015) studied the development of a tool based on the ARMA models to predict the demand for healthcare services.

ES are healthcare services that offer immediate care to a variety of patients. Consequently, the condition of a patient in the ES may vary from stable to highly critical. The classification of patients into different categories is very important for staff in order to ensure high-quality service at the operational level. In France, all ES use the same systems of classification: the CCMU, which indicates how serious a patient's condition is (impact on the resources required for the patient to be treated) and the GEMSA (a multi-center study group on reception services), which indicates the status of the patient after they have been through the ES (hospitalized, gone back home) (Panorama Urgences 2013). The forecasting of patient flows into the ES would be more useful if this was applied to each category of patients as this would provide decision-makers with a detailed forecast of the expected demand levels. A recent study by Kadri *et al.* (2014) has drawn attention to the importance of forecasting patient flow by category. However, this study focused on the GEMSA classification, which may help in predicting the number of beds needed for the hospitalization of patients in the pediatrics unit. Sun *et al.* (2009) have also studied the forecasting of patient flow into ES by category. They classified patients based on the level of seriousness of their condition and developed models to predict daily flows for each category.

5.3.3. *Summary*

Forecasting is a powerful tool present in several fields of application. The scientific community has explored the use and development of this tool since the early 19th Century. It has numerous fields of application, which are chiefly based on demand for a service.

The earliest projects that showed an interest in forecasting patient flows into emergency services date back to 1998, with the application of ARMA models used to predict arrivals into ES. Models that would be appropriate for the prediction of inflows into ES continued to be developed in recent years following the high demand for ES in modern hospitals.

The organization of ES has evolved greatly in recent years given the remarkable increase in demands for emergency care services. This has led to a diversification of cases that come into the ES and, thus, to the classification of patients depending on the severity of their condition. The method of forecasting for each patient category has recently drawn the attention of the scientific community and remains a promising support that could help ES staff to better understand the phenomenon of the arrival of patients into the ES.

5.4. Analysis of the inflows of patients into emergency care

In this section, we present the set of data that were collected from the information system (IS) used in the ES in the THC. We also present the statistical analysis carried out on these extracted data. The aim of this is to clarify the source and the nature of the data used in our study and to carry out a preliminary analysis.

5.4.1. *Data extraction*

Data extraction is the act or process through which data are retrieved from a source in order to be processed or to be stored. This process is usually followed by a transformation of these data and, sometimes, by the addition of meta-data before it can be used in subsequent steps. The majority of forecasting studies are based on a history of observation of the phenomenon.

Indeed, history is essential for analyzing the studied phenomenon and for extracting information on its behavior. In the context of our study, we were interested in the number of patients visiting the THC ES on a daily basis, this phenomenon being the subject of our study.

Since 2007, the THC has opted to digitize data on the flow of patients through their ES (Figure 5.3). Thus, staff have a tool allowing for the digital and time-stamped management of all actions related to patient care (arrival, examination by nursing staff, examination by the doctor, treatment, etc.).

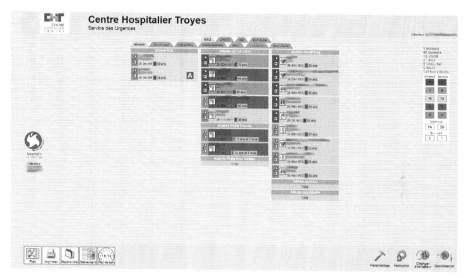

Figure 5.3. *ResUrgences: the digital management software for patients passing through the ES in the Troyes HC*

When the ResUrgences software was launched in 2007, emergency care staff entered into a migratory period – moving to the digitized tool to manage patient flows. This transition phase lasted for 2 years so that all the staff were able to use the software systematically and correctly. The duration was due to several factors such as: resistance to change, the complexity of the tool, and staff turnover. For all these reasons, the Medical Information Department in the THC believe that the database for this tool is reliable only from 2010 onward.

We have collected the Emergency Care Summary (ECS) for every patient between January 1, 2010 and December 21, 2014. There are a total of 252,438 entries. The ECS is a normalized collection of data used by all ES in France. It contains 20 fields of information that describe the patient's journey through the ES. The fields that are of greatest interest in our study are: the date time and entry, and the CCMU and GEMSA classifications (explained in the following section). All this information is entered and updated in the patient file when they have been treated in the service, depending on their final diagnosis. It is based on these data that we will carry out our forecasting of patient inflows.

The final result of our extraction is a table of data that contains the following three fields:

1) date of arrival in emergency care;

2) the CCMU classification;

3) the GEMSA classification.

5.4.2. *Data modeling*

The retrieved data are categorized into two classes: the clinical classification of the patients in emergency care (CCMU) and the multi-center study groups of reception services (GEMSA). The CCMU classification was developed by the Association for Research on Emergency Services (ARU) and has since been taken up by other scientific societies. This classification makes it possible to sort patients into different categories depending on the seriousness of their condition and the medical actions carried out. The GEMSA classification has been validated by the Commission of Emergency Medicine of the French Intensive Care Society. It sorts patients into 6 types of pathways through the ES. In principle, the nature of this trajectory is established *a posteriori*. The criteria for classification are: the mode of entry and departure of the patient and whether or not the care is planned. The GEMSA indicator thus makes it possible to trace the organization of the care administered and the patient's pathway.

The CCMU category indicates the seriousness of the condition of the patient, while the GEMSA category indicates the mode of admission and outcome for the patient after having received treatment within the ES. It gives necessary technical information for the treatment of the patient: the need for an MRI or X-ray, the need to carry out biological tests, treatment time by the doctor, the need for surgical intervention, the need for special consultation, etc.

The GEMSA classification differentiates between two chief categories: hospitalized patients and non-hospitalized patients. Regarding whether admission was planned or not, this has no impact on the management of patient flows. Indeed, patients who make planned visits to the ES are either patients transferred from another healthcare center, with information about the critical arrivals being shared by SAMU (the French emergency medical call center), or are patients who have been redirected from other emergency centers by an external doctor. In all cases, the ES staff is informed of the arrival of the patient a few hours in advance, at best, which can only help in planning activities at an operational level.

CCMU	Description
C1	Stable condition, no additional diagnostic or therapeutic action
C2	Stable condition, additional diagnostic or therapeutic action carried out
C3	Condition may worsen without resulting in death
C4	Prognosis pronounced, no immediate procedure for reanimation
C5	Prognosis pronounced, procedure for reanimation carried out immediately
CP	Patient presenting with dominant psychological or psychiatric problems in the absence of unstable somatic pathology
CD	The patient died upon arrival, without benefiting from the initiation or pursuit of emergency reanimation
CX	Unspecified

Table 5.2. *CCMU classification of patients in emergency care*

In conclusion, we can state that there are no planned arrivals in the ES in the short term (days) or the long term (weeks, months).

GEMSA	Mode of admission	Description
G1	Unplanned	Patient died or arrival or died before any reanimation procedure
G2	Unplanned	Patient not summoned, unexpected arrival of patient, patient returns home after administration of emergency care
G3	Planned	Patient summoned, arrival expected, returns home after administration of emergency care
G4	Unplanned	Patient not summoned, unexpected arrival, hospitalized after administration of emergency care
G5	Planned	Patient sumoned, arrival expected, hospitalized after administration of emergency care
G6	Unplanned	Patient requiring immediate or prolonged care (intensive care)
GX	Unspecified	Unspecified

Table 5.3. *GEMSA classification of patients in emergency care*

The different CCMU and GEMSA classifications and their explanations are given in Tables 5.2 and 5.3, respectively. The presence of certain categories with unspecified fields in both the CCMU and GEMSA classifications, which we have designated, respectively, by the notations CX and GX, are used in certain special cases. The CX category is attributed to a patient if:

1) the patient is a child. In this case, they are redirected toward the special pediatrics unit within the ES;

2) the patient departed without being examined by a doctor: the field is left empty as the patient received no diagnosis.

The data that were gathered were sorted by GEMSA and CCMU category and then transformed into time series representing the number of daily visits to the ES. Figures 5.4 and 5.5 indicate the number of daily arrivals by CCMU and GEMSA categories, in the ES of the THC, from January 2013 to December 2014.

5.4.3. *Descriptive statistics*

At first glance, the daily arrivals of patients in the ES of the THC, from 2010 to 2014, seem to show (Figure 5.4) that the majority of the arrivals are classified under C2, in the CCMU classification. Indeed, descriptive statistics (Table 5.4) for the CCMU category show that 75.44% of arrivals are categorized as C2. Moreover, the C1 and C2 categories (the less serious patients, see Table 5.2 for more details) represent a ratio of 86.09%, which signifies that the ES is often overpopulated by patients whose condition is not serious.

On the other hand, the daily number of arrivals chiefly fall into the G2 and G4 categories of the GEMSA classification. The G1 group represents the unplanned, external patients. This category groups together unplanned patients who return home after having received treatment in emergency care, while the second category (G4) groups together unplanned and hospitalized patients (see Table 5.3 for more details). Depending on the statistics for the GEMSA categories (Table 5.4), the categories G2 and G4 (unplanned patients) contain 93.35% of the total flow of patients in the ES, which confirms the random nature of the arrivals.

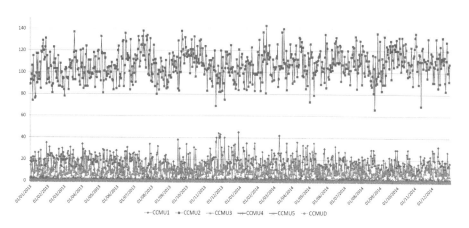

Figure 5.4. *View of the overall arrival of patients in the ES of the Troyes HC from 01/01/2010 to 31/12/2014 per category of CCMU. For a color version of this figure, see www.iste.co.uk/blua/hospital.zip*

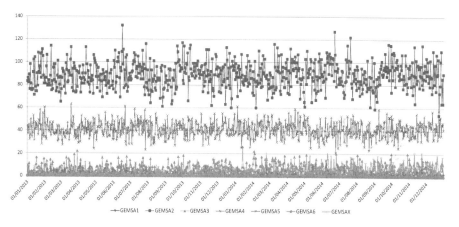

Figure 5.5. *View of the overall arrival of patients in the ES of the Troyes HC from 01/01/2010 to 31/12/2014 per category of GEMSA. For a color version of this figure, see www.iste.co.uk/blua/hospital.zip*

The variation in daily arrivals into the ES (Figures 5.4 and 5.5) indicates the absence of any definite trend. A slight seasonal trend may be observed during certain periods of the year. For example: there is a decrease in the summer and an increase at the start of the school year. As can be seen in the box plots for the daily number of arrivals by each category in the CCMU (Figure 5.6) and

GEMSA (Figure 5.7), the C1 and C2 categories (Figure 5.6) and the G2 and G4 categories (Figure 5.7) show the highest variations in the total flows in the ES. We can state here that forecasting for these categories (C1, C2, G2 and G4) is essential for an effective strategy to manage ES.

Category	Average	Minimum	Maximum	Standard deviation	Total (%)
C1	14.71	0	54	7.70	10.65
C2	104.17	45	177	14.11	75.44
C3	9.22	0	28	4.55	6.68
C4	0.98	0	7	1.02	0.71
C5	0.49	0	5	0.72	0.35
CD	0.08	0	2	0.27	0.05
CP	1.81	0	16	1.93	1.31
CX	6.64	0	40	5.01	4.81
G1	0.05	0	2	0.22	0.03
G2	86.37	41	146	12.76	62.55
G3	4.79	0	26	3.95	3.47
G4	42.53	14	81	7.43	30.80
G5	2.06	0	17	2.31	1.49
G6	0.16	0	3	0.42	0.12
GX	2.12	0	21	2.97	1.54
Total	138.09	65	238	15.42	100.00

Table 5.4. *Descriptive statistics for the daily inflow of patients per category of the CCMU and GEMSA*

The reason for introducing this new classification is to reduce the number of possible cases based on the patient's condition in emergency care and to classify patients from a perspective that is more practical for emergency care personnel.

5.5. Introduction of a new classification of patients in emergency care

In this section, we will present a new, practical classification of patients in ES which will group together the CCMU and GEMSA categories used by all emergency care services in France. This new classification is based on statistical tests carried out on data of arrivals in the ES of the THC over the last 5 years (2010–2014) and is based on the expertise of personnel (doctors and nurses) who use these classifications.

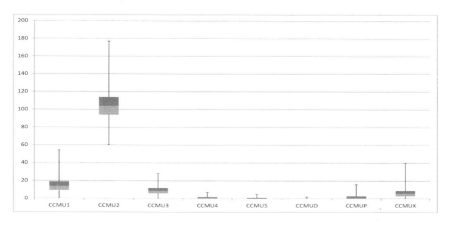

Figure 5.6. *Box plot for the number of arrivals per CCMU category. For a color version of this figure, see www.iste.co.uk/blua/hospital.zip*

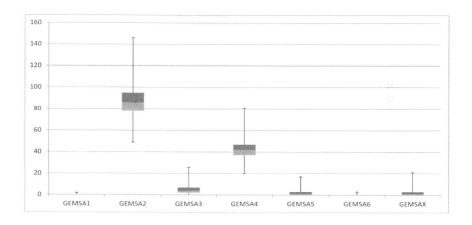

Figure 5.7. *Box plot for the number of arrivals per GEMSA category. For a color version of this figure, see www.iste.co.uk/blua/hospital.zip*

5.5.1. *Interest and motivation*

In the section where we described the data, we emphasized that the data retrieved had a CCMU and GEMSA field for each record that represented the pathway of a patient. However, we noted that the categories represent the same patient flows or, in other words, the categorization was redundant. This is one of the reasons that led us to introduce a new, practical classification that takes into account the CCMU and the GEMSA categories.

Forecasting a state of health or a situation for a population aggregate with a specific problem, or for groups from the same family, is not as complicated as forecasting this for an individual. This is because, by grouping the variances of the factors related to the population (which are generally large and well-known), the behavior of the aggregated data may possess very stable characteristics, even when individuals present high degrees of chance (Sanders 2001). It is, therefore, easier to obtain a greater degree of precision in forecasting specific health events when we use data for population distributions as compared to data for specific individuals.

5.5.2. *Statistical approach*

An important observation must be highlighted, with respect to the appearance of inconsistent states in the probability mass function table for crossed CCMU and GEMSA categories. For example, the state CD $\times$ G4 is produced 64 times but is a state that cannot occur in a patient (CD: dead on arrival in the ES; G4: hospitalized after administration of emergency care). This indicates the possibility of data that were wrongly entered by personnel, given that the IS does not allow us to prevent incompatible data entries.

5.5.3. *New classification: patient state*

This section presents a new practical classification of patients in emergency care. This new classification consists of grouping together the CCMU and GEMSA categories depending on the statistical texts and the expertise of the ES staff. We have called this new classification PS, for patient state. The cross-combinations of CCMU and GEMSA classifications reduce the number of states possible for a patient in the ES to a practical number of categories with a meaningful description of their pathway through the department.

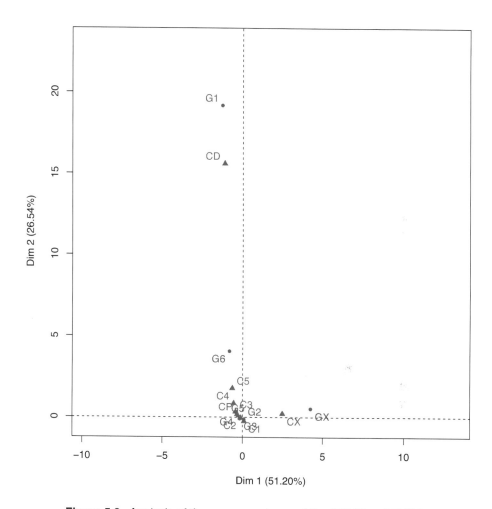

Figure 5.8. *Analysis of the correspondence of the CCMU × GEMSA contingency table. For a color version of this figure, see www.iste.co.uk/blua/hospital.zip*

Figure 5.9 presents the PS classification, which has 8 different attributes. Each category was created by grouping together several cross-combinations of the CCMU and GEMSA categories. Table 5.6 provides a description of each category. In the following sections we will discuss the arguments that motivated our choice of grouping for each PS category.

		CCMU							
		C1	C2	C3	C4	C5	CD	CP	CX
GEMSA	G1	0 %	0.0083 %	0.0032 %	0.0020 %	0.0044 %	0.0166 %	0 %	0 %
	G2	29.88 %	47.66 %	1.20 %	0.0503 %	0.0111 %	0.0044 %	0.43 %	3.26 %
	G3	0.26 %	3.06 %	0.13 %	0.0123 %	0.0028 %	0.0004 %	0.0044 %	0.0154 %
	G4	0.47 %	23.44 %	5.14 %	0.59 %	0.29 %	0.0265 %	0.84 %	0.0028 %
	G5	0.04 %	1.20 %	0.18 %	0.0246 %	0.0170 %	0.0004 %	0.0254 %	0 %
	G6	0.0012 %	0.0289 %	0.0206 %	0.0281 %	0.0309 %	0.0071 %	0.0004 %	0 %
	GX	0.0036 %	0.02 %	0.0008 %	0 %	0 %	0 %	0 %	1.57 %

Table 5.5. *Probability mass-function*
of the CCMU and GEMSA classifications

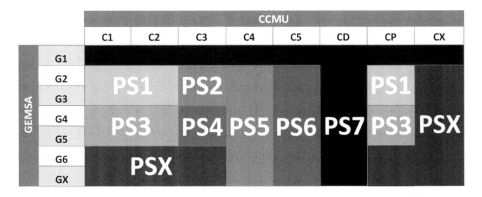

Figure 5.9. *PS classification of patients in emergency care. For a color*
version of this figure, see www.iste.co.uk/blua/hospital.zip

5.5.3.1. *PS1*

This category groups together the CCMU categories C1, C2 and CP crossed with the GEMSA categories G2 and G3 (see Figure 5.9). The C1 and C2 categories are used for a patient whose condition is considered stable. The only difference between these categories resides in whether or not an additional procedure is required (see Table 5.2). There is sometimes confusion over whether C1 or C2 is applicable when the data are entered in the IS. The chief reason for this is the loose definition of "additional procedure", which differentiates C2 from C1. This may lead to a difference in classification from one doctor to the next. The category PS1 also includes the category CP, which designates a patient with psychological problems. From a flow management point of view, a patient presenting with psychological problems requires the same quantity of resources as a patient in the C1 or C2 categories. The G2 and G3 categories are applicable to patients who have left the ES after having been treated. The difference between them resides in the mode of admission: G2 for an unplanned admission and G3 for a planned admission. To summarize: the PS1 category represents ambulatory patients who are given moderate medical treatment.

PS	Description
PS1	Patient leaving with moderate medical treatment
PS2	Patient leaving with serious medical treatment
PS3	Patient hospitalized having moderate medical treatment
PS4	Patient hospitalized with serious medical treatment
PS5	Patient requiring major medical treatment
PS6	Patient requiring major medical treatment + reanimation procedures
PS7	Patient deceased on arrival
PSX	Other

Table 5.6. *Description the PS classification of patients in emergency care*

5.5.3.2. *PS2*

This category consists of C3 crossed with the G2 and G3 categories (see Figure 5.9). The C3 category is applied to a patient when their condition is unstable and may worsen over time. This category of patients often needs immediate medical attention and may need to be rushed past the waiting area for immediate treatment. This often requires superior medical techniques than the PS1 category. By crossing the C3 category with the G2 and G3 categories (for the same reasons presented above) we arrive at a class of patients who require serious medical treatment.

5.5.3.3. *PS3*

This category groups together C1, C2 and CP (for the same reasons as with PS1) crossed with the G4 and G5 categories. This differs from PS1 in terms of the orientation of patients after they go through the ES – the PS3 category applies to patients who are hospitalized after treatment, either in the short-stay hospital unit, or in one of the major hospital units (cardiology, pulmonology, neurology, etc.). The PS3 category represents patients hospitalized after moderate medical treatment.

5.5.3.4. *PS4*

As with PS2, this category represents the class of ambulatory patients who require serious medical treatment.

5.5.3.5. *PS5*

This category covers the category of patients who have been redirected from another healthcare center or who have been admitted in to the ES as a result of a minor emergency accident (accident due to sports, a fall, etc.).This category of patients often requires greater care than the C1, C2 and C3 classes and generally requires the intervention of a specialist doctor or the need to carry out a minor intervention. This category represents patients who require major medical treatment.

5.5.3.6. *PS6*

This category groups together patients who were admitted into emergency care in a critical condition and require reanimation procedures.

5.5.3.7. *PS7*

This category is applicable to patients who were dead on arrival in the ES. It groups together CD crossed with the G1 category. Although we can note the presence of certain records with incoherent data entries, such as 11 entries in the CD $\times$ G2 category, which would correspond to a patient who was dead on arrival (CD) and who went back home after being treated in the ES (G2) – clearly an impossibility. Experts ascribe such records to incorrect usage of the IS. This was validated by carrying out a correspondence analysis with the probability mass function for the CCMU $\times$ GEMSA categories (Table 5.5). Correspondence analysis (CA) is a multivariate statistical technique which decomposes the $\tilde{\chi}^2$ statistic associated with a contingency table into orthogonal factors. A two-dimensional plot may help detect abnormal phenomena. Indeed, the CA diagram (Figure 5.8) of Table 5.5 indicates correlated abnormal behavior for CD and G1.

5.5.3.8. *PSX*

This category groups together the "unspecified" categories in the CCMU and GEMSA (CX and GX) along with the category G6. We chose to do this by taking into account the fact that the CX and GX categories had no impact on ES resources. It must also be noted that CX and GX have correlated abnormal behavior, as indicated in Figure 5.8. The G6 category was included because of its low occurrence (0.12%) and because this category represents the case of a serious condition where the patient is directly admitted into intensive care.

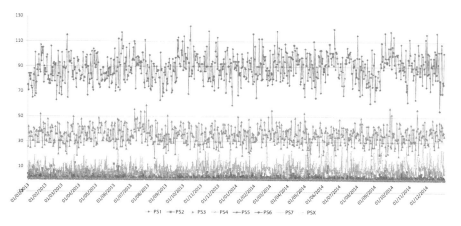

Figure 5.10. *Arrivals into emergency service by PS category from 01/01/2013 to 31/12/2014. For a color version of this figure, see www.iste.co.uk/blua/hospital.zip*

	Average	Standard deviation	Minimum	Maximum	Total (%)
PS1	84.73	12.12	48	132	61.29
PS2	1.84	1.95	0	15	1.33
PS3	35.96	7.15	16	69	26.01
PS4	7.35	3.97	0	25	5.31
PS5	0.97	1.02	0	7	0.70
PS6	0.48	0.72	0	5	0.35
PS7	0.10	0.32	0	2	0.07
PSX	6.81	5.08	0	40	4.93
Total	138.25	15.33	90	238	100.00

Table 5.7. *Descriptive statistics for the number of daily arrivals per PS category*

5.5.4. *Descriptive statistics for the new categories*

Figure 5.10 presents the daily arrivals into ES by PS category. This graph shows that the patient flow is chiefly classified as PS1 or PS3. It also indicates the absence of any trends in the given time-horizon. The descriptive statistics given in Table 5.7 confirm that PS1 and PS3 represent 87.30% of the total flow. The box plot given in Figure 5.11 indicates that the PS1 and PS3 categories have the largest variations in flow in the ES.

5.6. Forecast models for patient flows

5.6.1. *The process used in the study*

The process followed in a forecasting study consists of several steps that aim to make use of historical data from a given phenomenon in order to forecast the future. This is composed of four main phases.

5.6.1.1. *Retrieval*

Today, there are at least two kinds of information required: a) statistical data, and b) the collective expertise of the people of collect the data and use the forecasts. It is often difficult to obtain enough historical data to be able to adapt a good statistical model. However, from time to time, very old data are less useful given the changes in the studied phenomenon.

5.6.1.2. *Preliminary analysis (exploratory)*

We must always start by graphically representing the data. Do consistent models exist? Is there a significant trend? Is there a large seasonal variation? Is there evidence for the presence of economic cycles? Are there aberrant values in the data that must be explained by those with specialist knowledge? What is the force between the variables available for analysis? Different tools have been developed to help with this analysis.

5.6.1.3. *Choosing and adjusting models*

The best model to be used depends on the availability of historical data, the force of relationships between the forecasting variable and the explicative variables as well as the manner in which the forecasts will be used. It is common to compare two or three potential models. Each model is itself an artificial construction based on a set of hypotheses (explicit and implicit) and generally involves one or more parameters that must be "adjusted" by using known, historical data. In the following section, we will present some types of models that are the most widely used in literature.

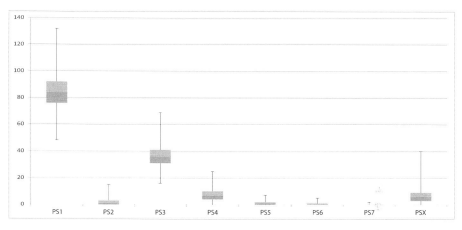

Figure 5.11. *Box plot for daily arrivals per PS category. For a color version of this figure, see www.iste.co.uk/blua/hospital.zip*

5.6.1.4. *Using and evaluating a forecasting model*

Once a model has been selected and its parameters estimated, the model is used in order to predict the phenomenon in the future. The model's performance can only be correctly evaluated when there are data available for the prediction period. A certain number of methods were developed to help evaluate the accuracy of the forecasts. There are, however, organizational problems in the use of these forecasting models as well as the action taken.

5.6.2. *Types of forecasting models*

5.6.2.1. *Basic models*

Certain forecasting methods are very simple and efficient. We present below certain methods that may be used as touchstones for other forecasting methods.

5.6.2.1.1. Forecasting using the mean

Here, all forecasts of all future values are equal to the mean of historical data. Let $y_1, y_2, ..., y_t$ be the historical observations for the phenomenon being studied. The forecast for the following period, denoted by P_{t+1} is given by the formula for the arithmetic mean:

$$P_{t+1} = \bar{y} = \frac{\sum_{i=1}^{t} y_i}{t} \tag{5.1}$$

5.6.2.1.2. Naive forecasting

This method is only appropriate for data in a time series. All forecasts are simply the value of the last observation. That is: the forecasts of all future values are y_t, where y_t is the last value observed. This method works remarkably well for many economic and financial time series.

$$P_{t+1} = y_t \tag{5.2}$$

5.6.2.1.3. Seasonal naive method

As the name indicates, this method is useful for highly seasonal phenomena. In this case, we define each forecast as being equal to the last value observed with respect to the same season of the year (e.g. the same month in the previous year). The forecasting in the period $t + h$ is, therefore, defined as follows:

$$P_{t+h} = y_{t+h-k\times m} \tag{5.3}$$

such that:

– m: seasonal periodicity;
– $k = \lfloor \frac{h-1}{m} \rfloor + 1$

5.6.2.1.4. Simple regression

The basic concept underlying this method is to predict a variable y by assuming that it is a linear relationship with another variable x. The model is called "simple" regression because only one explicative variable, x, is allowed. The simplest case is that of linear regression. The phenomenon y may be written and predicted as a function of the variable x in the following form:

$$y_t = a \times x_t + b + \epsilon_t \tag{5.4}$$

such that:

- a: the slop of the line that translates the correlation between y and x;

- b: the intercept;

- ϵ_t: the model error at the instant t.

5.6.2.1.5. Multiple regression

Unlike simple regression, this method seeks to explain (predict) a phenomenon based on several predictive variables. We can cite two examples of multiple regression, one based on transversal data and the other based on times series. The general form of a multiple regression is:

$$y_t = \beta_0 + \sum_{i=1}^{K} \beta_i \times x_{i,t} + \epsilon_t \qquad [5.5]$$

such that:

- $x_{i,t}$: explicative variable i for the period t, with $i \in 1..K$;

- β_i: coefficient of the explicative variable i;

- β_0: the intercept;

- ϵ_t: the model error at the instant t;

- the mean of the errors is zero;

- the errors are not auto-correlated;

- the errors are not correlated with the explicative variables x_i.

It is also useful if the errors are normally distributed with constant variance, in order to produce prediction intervals. However, this is not necessary for forecasting (Brockwell and Davis 2002).

5.6.2.1.6. Simple exponential smoothing

The simplest exponential smoothing method is, naturally, called "simple exponential smoothing" (SES). This method is useful for predicting phenomena without any trends or seasonal effect (Brockwell and Davis 2002). The principle of this method is to predict the phenomena based on the weighted mean between the most recent observation and the most recent forecast. The formula for this is the following:

$$P_t = \alpha \times y_{t-1} + (1 - \alpha)P_{t-1} \qquad [5.6]$$

which may also be expressed as follows:

$$P_t = P_{t-1} + \alpha \times \epsilon_{t-1} \qquad [5.7]$$

5.6.2.2. *Decomposition of time series*

Phenomena modeled as a time series may present behavior that can be divided into several components, each of which represents one of the categories of a related sub-phenomenon. We present certain models and common methods to extract associated components for a time series. This is often done to better understand the phenomenon and is also useful in improving the forecasts.

Seasonal and trend decomposition using loess (STL) (Cleveland *et al.* 1990) is a highly versatile and robust method for the decomposition of a chronological series, while loess is a method for estimating nonlinear relationships. The STL method was developed by Cleveland *et al.* (1990), and is based on the principle of decomposing a series of the following form:

$$y_t = F(T_t, S_t, C_t, \epsilon_t) \qquad [5.8]$$

such that:

– T_t: trend component;

– S_t: seasonal component;

– C_t: conjectural component;

– ϵ_t: model error.

We identify two decomposition models: an additive model and a multiplicative model (Yalaoui *et al.* 2012) whose equations are given using formulas 5.9 and 5.10, respectively.

$$y_t = T_t + S_t + C_t + \epsilon_t \qquad [5.9]$$

$$y_t = T_t \times S_t \times C_t \times \epsilon_t \qquad [5.10]$$

5.6.2.3. *ARIMA models*

The ARIMA models offer another forecasting approach for time series. Along with the exponential smoothing method, they are considered to be the most widely used methods for predicting time series and they provide additional approaches for carrying out forecasting. While the exponential smoothing models are based on a description of trends and seasonality in data, the ARIMA models aim to describe the auto-correlations in the data.

ARIMA is, in a way, a combination of two models: the AR model that uses the regression of the variable against the variable itself up to a certain order, denoted by p (formula [5.11]) and the MA, which, rather than using historical values of the phenomenon, uses forecasting errors in the past up to a certain order, denoted by q, in a regression type model (formula [5.12]).

$$y_t = c + \epsilon_t + \sum_{i=1}^{p} \phi_i y_{t-i} \qquad [5.11]$$

$$y_t = c + \epsilon_t + \sum_{j=1}^{q} \theta_j \epsilon_{t-j} \qquad [5.12]$$

The final formula for the ARIMA model is a combination of the two models presented above and this takes the following form:

$$y_t = \sum_{i=1}^{p} \phi_i y_{t-i} + \sum_{j=1}^{q} \theta_j \epsilon_{t-j} + \epsilon_t + c \qquad [5.13]$$

5.6.2.4. *Time horizons for forecasts*

The time horizon for a forecast refers to how far ahead in time the period is for which we wish to predict. This could be over the short term, the medium term or the long term. There are no clearly defined limits for the time horizons in the field of hospitals in literature. However, by borrowing the classification common to other disciplines, such as financial, commercial or econometric forecasts, a short-term forecast could refer to a period over one day or a quarter of a year. A medium-term forecast covers a period of a quarter of a year to a year, and long-term forecasts refer to a period of 1 year or 5 years, at most. Nonetheless, these horizons are not appropriate for all situations and may instead be defined with respect to the qualitative forecasting indicator. In our case, we have developed two forecasting models: a long-term model to predict the annual activity of the ES and a short-term model to improve the forecasting up to a day by integrating recent observations.

– *Long-term forecasting model*: this type of model is used to forecast a phenomenon over a long-term time horizon. They are very useful from a strategic point of view as they offer decision-makers a global overview of the expected activity over the long term, which will, consequently, enable them to adjust their strategic plans. Models of these type are generally constructed using only exogenous data (e.g. time index, day of the week, special events, etc.). That is, they express the phenomenon (e.g. demand or weather) based only on exogenous data.

– *Short-term forecasting model*: this type of model is used to predict a phenomenon in the near future. They are often used to take tactical decisions as they may be better-performing than long-term forecasting models. These models are generally constructed using recent observations of the phenomenon itself and the errors made by the forecasting model. This is generally the goal of models such as the ARIMA model.

5.6.3. *Choosing classes to predict*

The ABC method (also known as Pareto) classes elements based on their importance in a given study. This consists of sorting elements into three classes (A, B or C) depending on a criterion. The choice of criterion determines the importance of each element in the study. As a general rule, the classes correspond to the following percentages:

– class A: an element found in a small percentage of the population (10–20%), representing a high value for the criterion (70–80%);

– class B: an element found in a moderate percentage of the population (20–40%), representing an average value for the criterion (15–28%);

– class C: an element found in a large percentage of the population (40–60%) representing a small value for the criterion (2–5%).

In order to determine the percentage of each category in the ABC classification, we calculate the discrimination rate, denoted by DR. The percentage of the classes A, B and C is then deduced based on its value. For more information on these methods, please refer to (Yalaoui *et al.* 2012, p. 163).

In this study, the criterion used to classify the PS categories is the occurrence of each category. This decision was taken based on the fact that it is more important to focus on the categories of patients who frequent the ES the most. Table 5.8 represents the result of the ABC classification of the PS categories. The percentage of each class has been deduced from the DR, calculated as indicated in Figure 5.12. In this case, the DR is equal to 78.97%, which signifies that the percentage of each class is 20% for the classes A and B and 60% for C class.

PS	Occurrence	Frequency (%)	Cumulative frequency (%)	ABC class
1	157,488	61.25	61.25	A
3	66,775	25.97	87.22	A
4	13,652	5.31	92.53	B
X	12,884	5.01	97.54	B
2	3,429	1.33	98.88	C
5	1,800	0.70	99.58	C
6	894	0.35	99.93	C
7	190	0.07	100.00	C

Table 5.8. *ABC analysis of the PS classes*

The ABC classification indicates that the PS1 and PS3 categories are those which have the greatest impact on the patients flows into the ES. This has been derived from Table 5.8, indicating that these belong to class A in the ABC classification. Our forecasting models are then applied to these two categories in parallel with the total patient traffic. We have also considered the sum of the PS1 and PS3 categories, as they make up 87.22% of the final flow.

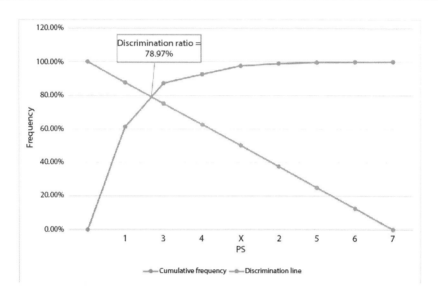

Figure 5.12. *ABC analysis curve for the PS category. For a color version of this figure, see www.iste.co.uk/blua/hospital.zip*

5.6.4. *Adjusted long-term forecasting model*

The long-term forecasting models have been developed to give decision-makers a global view of patient flows over 1 year. In the hospital world, the phenomenon of demand for a health service is often influenced by certain period fluctuations (long-term as well as short-term) associated with other characteristics. They are described as being cyclic. Seasonality is also a cyclic phenomenon, but one that is related to annual events and is described as a predictable and repetitive position around a trend line. A major difference between cyclic models and seasonal models is that the former varies in length and height with respect to the latter. Chatfield (2016) describes how seasonality and cyclicity may be evaluated in either the additive or multiplicative form.

The chief objective of long-term forecasting models is to predict a given phenomenon over a long-term time horizon (n periods in the future) and this is usually done using the decomposition of the time series method presented in equation [5.8]. The chief components that interest us are:

– *trend*: a trend describes the evolution of the phenomenon over time (stable, increasing or decreasing);

– *conjuncture*: the conjunctural component describes the effect of special events on the evolution of the phenomenon. For example, the effect of times of epidemics on the daily arrival of patients into ES;

– *seasonality*: this represents fluctuations with a constant periodicity (week, month, quarter, etc.);

– *residual*: this represents a random component of the phenomenon, which cannot be described using any of the other components discussed above.

Let y_t denote the time series that represents the daily number of patients in the ES for a given category (PS1, PS3 or the total). Developing a model for the decomposition of the time series consists of expressing y_t as a function of the different components presented above (equation [5.8]).

Choosing the appropriate model among the two presented earlier (additive 5.9 or multiplicative 5.10) in order to adapt to a phenomenon depends on its nature. Additive models are appropriate for phenomena with a constant seasonal amplitude over time, while multiplicative models are appropriate for phenomena that have a variable seasonal change (amplified or reduced each season) (see (Chatfield 1993; Yalaoui *et al.* 2012)). As we can see in Figure 5.10, the daily patient flow in the ES does not present an amplified or diminished seasonality over time (it is flattened). Consequently, the most appropriate model for our case is the additive model.

5.6.4.1. *Estimation of the trend component*

The trend component describes the evolution of the phenomenon over time. This evolution may be represented as a linear dependency between the observation and the time index, t (Yalaoui *et al.* 2012), using the following formula:

$$T_t = a \times t + b \qquad [5.14]$$

The optimal parameters of this equation are denoted by $\hat{a}$ and $\hat{b}$ and they minimize the mean square error between the observation y_t and the trend component T_t. They are calculated using the least squares method (Yalaoui *et al.* 2012). They have the following formulas:

$$\hat{a} = \frac{cov(t, y_t)}{var(t)} \qquad [5.15]$$

$$\hat{b} = mean(y_t) - \hat{a} \times mean(t) \qquad [5.16]$$

5.6.4.2. *Estimation of the seasonal component*

The first step in estimating the seasonal component of the additive model is to identify, using graphical analysis, the periodicity of the phenomenon. Let m be the number of observations in the season and let N be the total number of seasons. The seasonal coefficients, S_t, are calculated for each period of the season using equation [5.18].

$$S_t = y_t - T_t \qquad\qquad [5.17]$$

$$\bar{S}_t = \frac{\sum_{i=0}^{N-1} S_{t+i\times n}}{N} \qquad\qquad [5.18]$$

In our case study, we observed a specific kind of seasonality, which follows the day of the week and the weeks of the year. The seasonality relative to the week in the year is due to the distribution of residents of the Troyes commune because of recurrent events such as public holidays, the school year, epidemics (usually occurring in weeks 5, 6, and 7). The seasonality relative to the day of the week is due to human behavior, which prefers a visit to the ES at the beginning of the week. Figure 5.13 presents the superimposition of the total daily flows into the ES for the week and for days of the week.

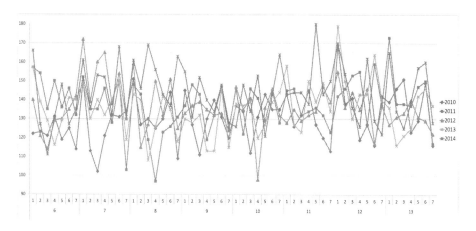

Figure 5.13. *The daily flows of patients from weeks 45 to 48 are superimposed. For a color version of this figure, see www.iste.co.uk/blua/hospital.zip*

5.6.5. *Short-term forecasting models*

In this section, we present the models used to generate short-term forecasting models. We have used the ARMA models, which are very effective for exploring the recent historical observations of a phenomenon in order to predict its behavior in the near future. The autoregressive (AR) part of this model describes the dependency of an observation on earlier measurements up to a time gap that is usually denoted by p, while the MA part describes the impact of earlier errors up to a defined time interval usually denoted by q, and the general formulation of an ARMA model is given by equation [5.13] (see (Brockwell and Davis 2002) for more details on the ARMA/ARIMA models).

In our case study, the component for which we adapted an ARMA model is the residual component of the long-term model (equation [5.9]). From this, we define the random variable $R(t)$:

$$R(t) = Y^*(t) - T(t) - \bar{S}(t) \tag{5.19}$$

The first step in developing an ARMA model is to identify the dependency lag between the phenomenon and the preceding observations i.e., identifying the parameters (p, q) for the model. The order of the auto-correlation parameter, p, corresponds to the number of significant peaks in the partial auto-correlation function (PACF) of the data. The auto-correlation function (ACF) gives the order of the MA parameter, q, of the model (see (Brockwell and Davis 2002) for more details on the ARMA models).

The second step, following that of identifying the parameters (p, q) is to estimate the parameters a_i and b_j such that the residuals of the ARMA models follow a given distribution. In general, the residuals are assumed to follow a normal law, with a mean of zero and standard deviation that must be minimized. The maximum likelihood method is the most widely used method in literature to estimate these parameters. It aims to maximize the statistical resemblance of errors to a given distribution. In the case of a normal distribution, this is the same as minimizing the sum of the squared errors of the ARMA model (Brockwell and Davis 2002).

The residuals of the long-term model, $(R(t))$, are thus modeled and may be predicted by an ARMA process as follows:

$$R^*(t) = \sum_{i=1}^{p} a_i R_{t-i} + \sum_{j=1}^{q} b_j \varepsilon_{t-j} + \varepsilon_t \qquad [5.20]$$

The short-term forecast of the phenomenon is, thus, given by the following equation:

$$Y^{**}(t) = T(t) + \bar{S}(t) + \sum_{i=1}^{p} a_i R_{t-i} + \sum_{j=1}^{q} b_j \varepsilon_{t-j} + \varepsilon_t \qquad [5.21]$$

5.7. Tests and implementation of the models

5.7.1. *Testing the performance of the models*

In this section, we present the results of tests on forecast models constructed using the data on arrivals between January 2010 and December 2013, which we tested using the data from 2014. We discuss the performance of the long-term and short-term forecasting models and the analysis of the residuals. The performance of the models is evaluated using the criterion of the relative mean percentage (RMAP) given by equation [5.25]. The authors have chosen to present the performance of models using this criterion as it gives a simple and intuitive interpretation of the performance of the models. The models have also been evaluated with respect to the Akaike Information Criterion (AIC) (see (Hirotugu 1974; Brockwell and Davis 2002) in the process of estimating the parameters of the models. A residual analysis was also carried out in order to test the null hypothesis of the distribution of white noise. Finally, we tested the presence of a correlation between the residuals and the epidemic cases in the Champagne–Ardenne region. While the correlation is insignificant (< 0.1), this means that the forecasting model is robust for a period in which there is an epidemic.

$$\varepsilon_t = Y_t - P_t \qquad [5.22]$$

$$MAE = mean|\varepsilon_t| \qquad [5.23]$$

$$RMAE = \frac{MAE}{mean(Y_t)} \qquad [5.24]$$

$$RMAP = 1 - RMAE \qquad [5.25]$$

– Y_t : the observation of daily arrivals on the day t;

– P_t : forecast of the daily arrivals on the day t;

– ε_t : the forecasting error for the day t;

– AME : the absolute mean of the errors;

– $RMAE$: the relative mean of the errors;

– $RMAP$: relative mean performance.

The results for the long-term and short-term forecasting models for the categories PS1, PS3, PS1 + PS3 and the total patient flow, constructed based on data from the years 2010 to 2013, and tested in 2014, are represented in Figures 5.14–5.16, respectively. From these figures, it can be observed that the long-term forecasting model follows the general trend of the observation for each category. The short-term model uses recent information on observations to improve the long-term forecasting. It can be seen that the short-term models tend to adjust the forecast in the case of a peak indicating an increase or fall (see Figures 5.14–5.16).

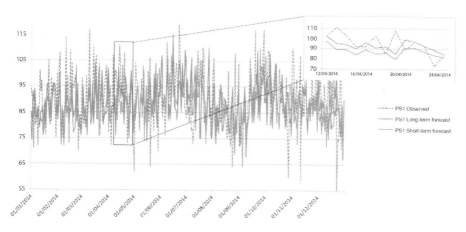

Figure 5.14. *Forecast for the PS1 category from 01/01/2014 to 31/12/2014 . For a color version of this figure, see www.iste.co.uk/blua/hospital.zip*

Table 5.9 indicates the performance of the long-term and short-term forecasting models for each category. We can see that the short-term models perform slightly better than the long-term models. This will help decision-makers anticipate a period of high rise in patient flows. We also note that the effectiveness of the models decreases from PS1 + PS3 to the 'total' category, which signifies that the PS1 and PS3 categories are the chief categories for patient flow into the ED, while the remaining categories (PS2, PS4, PS5, PS6, PS7 and PSX) are more likely to be random phenomena.

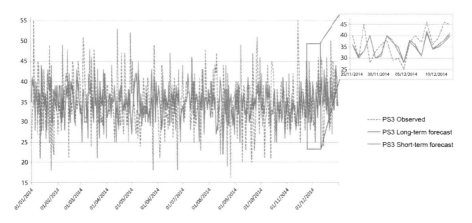

Figure 5.15. *Forecast for the PS3 category from 01/01/2014 to 31/12/2014. For a color version of this figure, see www.iste.co.uk/blua/hospital.zip*

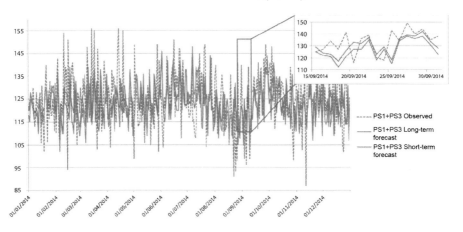

Figure 5.16. *Forecast for the PS1 + PS3 category from 01/01/2014 to 31/12/2014. For a color version of this figure, see www.iste.co.uk/blua/hospital.zip*

	RMAP	
	Long-term	Short-term
PS1	89.51%	90.20%
PS3	80.60%	81.29%
PS1 + PS3	91.63%	92.29%
Total	91.08%	91.84%

Table 5.9. *How the models perform*

5.7.2. *Analysis of the residuals*

In order to evaluate the quality of a forecasting models, the residuals of this model must be tested for a null hypothesis concerning white noise. White noise is the set of values observed for independent, random variables that are identically distributed and that follow the normal distribution, with a mean of zero and finite variance (Box and Jenkins 1971). This indicates that the series contains no auto-correlated information that may be used to predict future values. The first step consists of testing the white noise hypothesis for residuals and verifying the normality of these data. This may be carried out using a $\tilde{\chi}^2$ test (Brockwell and Davis 2002) or through visual tools such as the P-P and histograms. Figure 5.17 presents the P-P diagrams and histograms for the residuals of the PS1, PS1 + PS3 and total flow forecasting models. On the one hand, the numbers show that there is a perfect fit between the Gaussian distribution and the residuals of total flow forecasting. On the other hand, we see that the residuals for the PS1 forecasts have a poorer fit with the Gaussian distribution, which signifies that the forecasting model for this category may be improved by including data that are external to this model. The second step in testing the null hypothesis on white noise is to verify the number of deviations from the normal distribution in the ACF diagram for the residual sample.

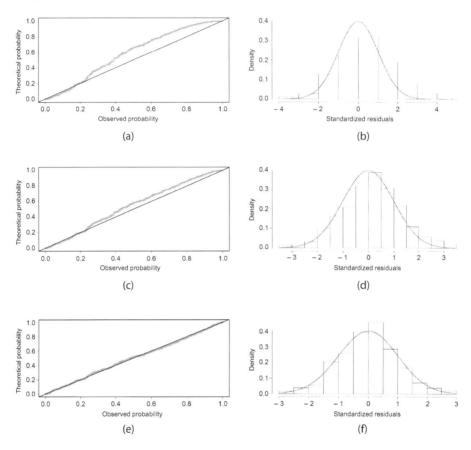

Figure 5.17. *Test of normality for the residuals of the flow models for PS1, PS1 + PS3 and the total: P-P (a,c,e) graphs, histograms (b,d,f)*

A sharper test for the null hypothesis on white noise is the Ljung-Box test which consists of testing the convergence of given statistical data with the $\tilde{\chi}^2$ distribution (Brockwell and Davis 2002). The values of p for this test are 0.86, 0.91 and 0.97 for residuals of the short-term forecasting models for the PS1, PS1 + PS3 and total flux categories, respectively. This indicates that the residues of all the models may be considered to be white noise.

5.7.3. *Analysis of the robustness of the model: epidemics*

In this section, we present a test for the correlation between the residuals of the long-term forecasting models in the PS1 + PS3 category and the cases of epidemics in the Champagne–Ardenne region. The epidemic data used in this study were retrieved from the online platform Sentinelles, a French organization that monitors epidemics in the country (source: the Sentinelles networks, INSERM/UPMC). We collected epidemiological data on flu and acute diarrhea between 01/01/2010 and 31/12/2014. To compare these data with the residuals of the forecasting model, we had to normalize these variables, as they were of differing orders of magnitude. Equation [5.26] shows how to obtain the normalized variable, Z, for a variable X:

$$Z = \frac{X - \mu}{\sigma} \qquad\qquad [5.26]$$

such that:

μ : the mean of X;

σ : the standard deviation X.

Figure 5.18 presents a line graph for the normalized residuals of a long-term forecasting model for the PS1 + PS3 category, along the standardized graph for flu and acute diarrhea. This graph shows that there is no visual correlation between them, which means that the epidemics do not affect the quality of the forecasting. Further, Table 5.10 shows a weak correlation between the residuals and epidemics. It can be concluded that the forecasting model is robust in the case of epidemics.

	Residuals	Flu	Acute diarrhea
Residuals	1	0.055	0.050
Flu	0.055	1	0.298
Acute diarrhea	0.050	0.298	1

Table 5.10. *Matrix showing the residuals × flu × acute diarrhea correlation*

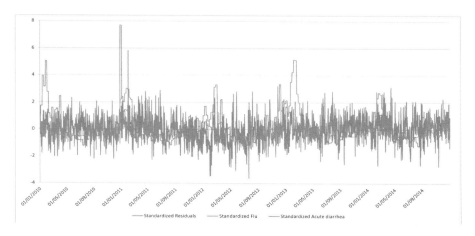

Figure 5.18. *Graph of the standardized graph of residual, flu and acute diarrhea from 01/01/2014 to 31/12/2014. For a color version of this figure, see www.iste.co.uk/blua/hospital.zip*

5.8. Application used in the ES of the THC: OptaUrgences®

5.8.1. *Introduction*

The role of this application is to provide an appropriate steering tool for ES in the THC. Indeed, in most cases the emergency service is the point of entry for patients into the hospital. This position of interface between the hospital and civil society poses several problems in correctly steering the activity in this department: this is both for reasons of patient flow forecasting as well as in the evaluation of the duration of treatment for patients. The chief goal of this application is to forecast patient flows in the different categories and to present them in a dedicated, ergonomic interface to the emergency staff, in particular, as well as to the heads of the other services. In this context, the first goal was that of developing a clear design brief that defined the different operational and non-operational requirements, as well as the input/output functions and the link with other ISs.

5.8.2. *Specifications*

5.8.2.1. *Operational needs*

Operational needs represent the chief function that the application must fulfill in order to carry out its role. The functional needs of our application are:

– identifying users who have permission to access the application;

– displaying a dashboard with patient flow forecasts: total/hospitalized/ non-hospitalized for the current day and the following day;

– displaying the weekly patient flow forecasts (total/hospitalized/non-hospitalized) for the present week, displayed as a table as well as in the form of a graph;

– displaying monthly flow forecasts for the present month of the year;

– printing out forecast sheets (daily, weekly);

– connecting to the internal database of each department to retrieve the most recent data in order to improve short-term forecasts;

– daily and annual updates of the forecast models.

This application must also distinguish between two types of users: a user and an administrator. This must be done in order to limit the modification functions available to users and for the updating of the forecasting models for personnel with administration privileges on the system. Figure 5.19 presents a diagram explaining the use of the application.

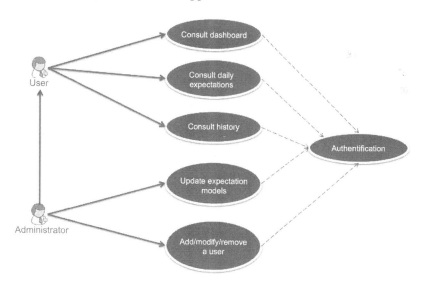

Figure 5.19. *Diagram explaining the use of the application. For a color version of this figure, see www.iste.co.uk/blua/hospital.zip*

5.8.2.2. *Main functions*

5.8.2.2.1. Displaying a dashboard

This function allows for a quick, general overview of the patient flow forecasts. The dashboard must include, within a single interface, the forecast for the present day and for the following day, as well as the patient flows observed on the previous day. This will allow the ES to have an idea of the kind of flows to expect as well as of the recent activity of the service. The dashboard must also display a forecast for the total patient flow for the present week, in order to give personnel an idea of the weekly changes in patient flow. Figure 5.20 presents the functional flowchart for this function.

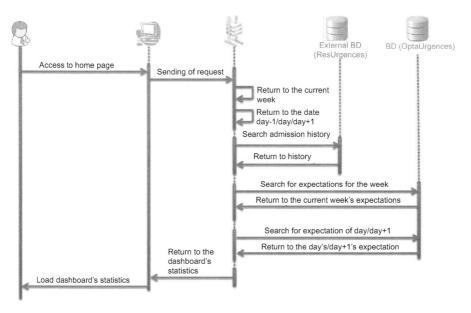

Figure 5.20. *Flowchart for consulting the dashboard. For a color version of this figure, see www.iste.co.uk/blua/hospital.zip*

5.8.2.2.2. Displaying the forecasts for a given day

This function must allow the display of the detailed forecasts for the different patient categories for a given day: the value forecast, the lower and upper limits of the forecast.

5.8.2.2.3. Displaying the forecasts for a week

This function must allow the display of detailed forecasts for the different patient categories for a given week: the value forecast, the lower and upper limits of the forecast for all days of the week. Figure 5.21 presents the flowchart for this function.

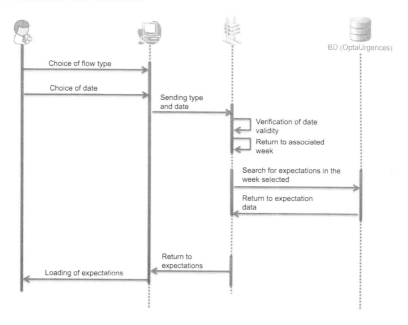

Figure 5.21. *Flowchart for the consultation of weekly forecasts. For a color version of this figure, see www.iste.co.uk/blua/hospital.zip*

5.8.2.2.4. Consulting history

This function allows the visualization of the history of the actual observations and of the forecasts for the different patient categories. This will allow the decision-maker to track the performance of the models and to evaluate their robustness in periods with high fluctuation. Figure 5.22 presents the flowchart for this function.

5.8.2.2.5. Updating forecasting models

This function must allow the updating of forecasting models, as discussed in section 5.6. The application must, thus, update the models based on the history of observations and, using this, it must calculate the new coefficients for the long-term or short-term models. Figure 5.23 presents the flowchart for this function.

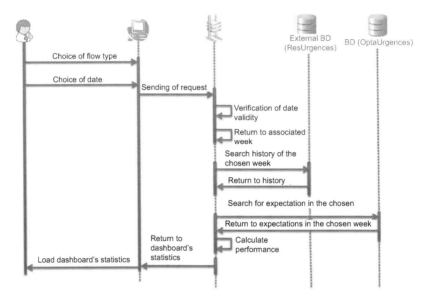

Figure 5.22. *Flowchart for the consultation of the forecast history. For a color version of this figure, see www.iste.co.uk/blua/hospital.zip*

5.8.2.3. *Liaison with the ES information system*

The functionality of updating the forecast models and that of displaying historical data require the retrieval of recent observations (long-term and short-term) of data on patients, in order to fulfill their role. As indicated in section 5.4, which discussed the analysis of patient flows, our source of data is the IS used in the THC ES. However, this software does not allow standardized electronic data interchange for data on patients passing through the ES. It has, therefore, proven necessary to directly retrieve these data from the database used by the IS, using SQL language, which allows total flexibility over the type and nature of the data retrieved.

This approach also makes it possible to extend the application to any IS used to retrieve data. This will allow the application to be quickly adopted in other ES.

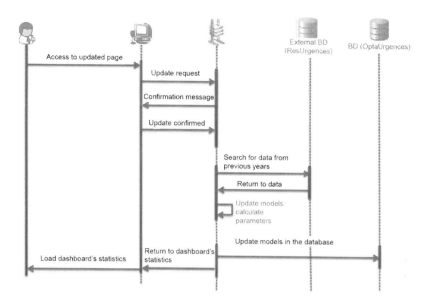

Figure 5.23. *Flowchart for the updating of forecast models. For a color version of this figure, see www.iste.co.uk/blua/hospital.zip*

5.8.3. *Implementation: development of algorithms*

The development of algorithms that allow us to calculate the coefficients for long-term and short-term forecast models is an important part of putting in place an application. Forecast models supply the database with predicted values for each patient category. This will subsequently be used by the different functions of the application.

These models were developed using two programming languages: Java and R (forecast library). The combination of these two languages offers the flexibility of integration with any programming interface via the Java package and also makes it possible to harness the power of the R software, dedicated to data analysis.

5.8.3.1. *A dedicated application for ES*

A professional application was developed for the THC in order to facilitate the implementation of and the use of forecasting algorithms. This application was called "Opta-Urgences" and was developed by the company[1]. The application integrated ergonomic display modules that allowed staff to easily interpret the forecasts.

To facilitate the visualization and interpretation of forecasts, the application displays the forecast for one day in the form of a gauge (Figure 5.24), indicating the predicted value and the limits using green, yellow and red to indicate the intensity of the predicted flow.

The application has also integrated green, yellow and red smiley faces (after the predictions) on a monthly calendar (Figure 5.26) to indicate the intensity of the flow on the concerned day.

5.8.4. *Example of the use of this application*

In this section, we will present an example for the use of this application which was put in place within the ES of the THC.

5.8.4.1. *Daily forecasts*

The daily forecast is used to detail the forecast of patient flows for a given day. It makes it possible to visualize the predicted values for the total flow and PS3 + PS4 (hospitalized patients) categories, showing their lower and upper limits. It also makes it possible to visualize the forecasts in the form of a gauge indicating green, yellow and red zones. This information can be extracted in a standard Excel or PDF format, for sharing between the ES staff. Figure 5.24 illustrates an example of the interface for a daily forecast.

5.8.4.2. *Weekly forecasts*

The weekly forecast makes it possible to visualize the forecasts over a given week in the form of a graph. It makes it possible to detail the predicted values for patients flow for the total flow and PS3 + PS4 (hospitalized patients categories, giving their lower and upper limits in the form of a table.

It is also possible to extract this information in a standard Excel or PDF format, for sharing between the ES staff. Figure 5.25 gives an example of the weekly forecast interface.

---

1 http://www.opta-lp.com/.

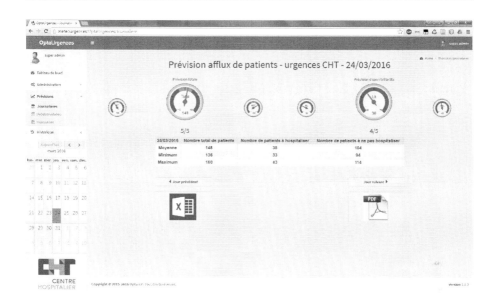

Figure 5.24. *Display interface for daily forecasts*

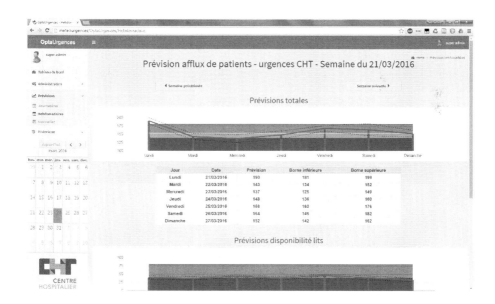

Figure 5.25. *Display interface for weekly forecasts*

5.8.4.3. *Monthly forecasts*

Monthly forecasts allow an overview of the predicted total flow and PS3 + PS4 flow for a month. The forecasts are presented in the form of a monthly calendar containing the predicted value for the total flow for each day, a smiley face that is green, yellow or red, indicating the intensity of the predicted flows, and an icon in the form of a bed in green or red, indicating whether the predicted number of hospitalized patients (PS3) exceeds the number of available beds in the short stay hospitalization unit (SSHU) of the ES. Figure 5.26 shows an example of the monthly forecast interface.

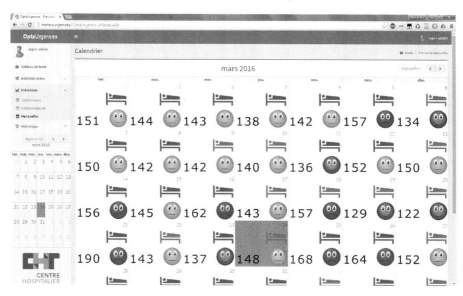

Figure 5.26. *Display interface of monthly forecasts*

5.8.5. *History of the performances*

The module analyzing the history of the performances makes it possible to compare the forecasts provided by the models with the actual flows observed in a given period. This makes it possible to trace a curve for the forecasts and their lower and upper limits, as well as the observed flows for the total and PS3 categories. This also indicates the performance of this model in this period and the mean flow observed. Figure 5.27 gives an example of the monthly forecast interface.

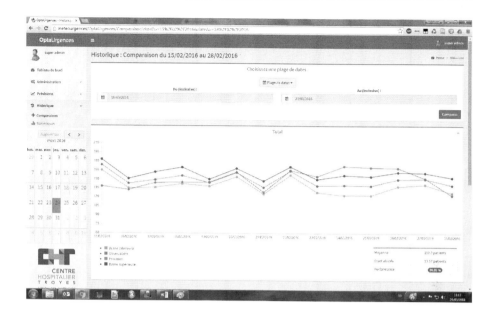

Figure 5.27. *Interface comparing observations and forecasts*

5.9. Conclusion

In this chapter, we studied the daily arrivals into the ES in the hospital center in the city of Troyes. We introduced a new, practical classification system for patients, which groups together patients with a similar behavior or requiring the same quantity of resources in the ES. By using time series analysis, we have developed forecast models for these newly introduced categories in order to help the ES staff plan their long-term and short-term activities.

The new classification of patients in the ES was introduced on the strength of statistical tests and the experience of ES staff. This new classification aimed to group together patients showing similar behavior into new categories (different from those already in use by all ES patients in France: CCMU and GEMSA). The resulting classification, called the PS (patient state), has reduced the number of ES patient categories from 58 to 8 possible states. This classification will help ES staff better understand their patient flows.

Based on the data analyzed for the period between January 2010 and December 2013, we developed long-term and short-term forecast models for the most important PS categories. The resulting models tested on the data from January 2010 to December 2014 have shown that these are high-performing models. We later tested the correlation of the residuals using the forecasting models and in the case of epidemics in order to examine the robustness of models during epidemics. We discovered that the correlation between these is insignificant. The forecasting models that we developed for our case study may be extended and used in other, similar ES, as they have proven to be adaptable to all categories of patient flow. These models are now used in the THC to predict the daily arrival of patients in the ES.

We also studied the possibility of using external data, such as data from calendars (holidays, special events, etc.) and meteorological measurements, as was recommended in a similar study (Kadri *et al.* 2014) to improve the quality of the forecasts. We had promising results for certain patient categories. We also presented the steps for developing and implementing a forecasting tool meant for the THC ES. The ergonomics of this tool is an important feature that facilitates the use of these forecasts by medical staff.

The tool presented here became available to administrative staff from March 2016 onward. Using the different display modules for historical data, a staff member manages the ES by adapting its capacity to welcome new patients based on the forecasts. The models had a performance rate of 91% from 01/03/2016 to 01/09/2017 (using the performance criterion defined by equation [5.25]).

Tracking the performance of the staff helped us identify certain forecasting errors, which corresponded to events specific to the commune of Troyes, which reduced or increased patient flows (general practitioner unavailable, weather conditions, etc.). This opened up a path to improve the forecast models by integrating an external variable, which will identify a period of low or high flows. This would be integrated as a calender in which the administrative staff share information on their prediction and it will be integrated using the X = ARMA in the calculation for short-term forecasting.

5.10. References

Aal, R.E.A. (2008). Univariate modeling and forecasting of monthly energy demand time series using abductive and neural networks. *Computers & Industrial Engineering*, 54(4), 903–917.

Aboagye Sarfo, P., Mai, Q., Sanfilippo, F.M., Preen, D.B., Stewart, L.M., Fatovich, D.M. (2015). A comparison of multivariate and univariate time series approaches to modelling and forecasting emergency department demand in Western Australia. *Journal of Biomedical Informatics*, 57, 62–73.

Ajmi, I., Zgaya, H., Hammadi, S. (2013). Optimized workflow for the healthcare logistic: Case of the pediatric emergency department. In *Optimization and Decision Science: Methodologies and Applications*, Sforza, A., Sterle, C. (eds). Springer, Berlin, 77–84.

Aksu, C., Gunter, S.I. (1992). An empirical analysis of the accuracy of SA, OLS, ERLS and NRLS combination forecasts. *International Journal of Forecasting*, 8(1), 27–43.

Atallah, H.Y., Lee, E.K. (2003). Modeling and optimizing emergency department workflow. Thesis, University School of Medicine, Atlanta.

Banerjee, A., Deaton, A., Duflo, E. (2004). Health, health care, and economic developement. *The American Economic Review*, 94(2), 326–330.

Bates, J.M., Granger, C.W.J. (1969). The combination of forecasts. *OR*, 20(4), 451–468.

Bergs, J., Heerinckx, P., Verelst, S. (2014). Knowing what to expect, forecasting monthly emergency department visits: A time-series analysis. *International Emergency Nursing*, 22(2), 112–115.

Bianchi, L., Jarrett, J., Hanumara, R.C. (1998). Improving forecasting for telemarketing centers by ARIMA modeling with intervention. *International Journal of Forecasting*, 14(4), 497–504.

Bouleux, G., Marcon, E., Mory, O. (2014). Early index for detection of pediatric emergency department crowding. *IEEE Journal of Biomedical and Health Informatics*, 99, 1.

Box, G.E.P., Jenkins, G.M. (1971) Time series analysis, forecasting and control. *Journal of the Royal Statistical Society. Series A*, 134(3), 450.

Boyle, J., Wallis, M., Jessup, M., Crilly, J., Lind, J., Miller, P., Fitzgerald, G. (2008). Regression forecasting of patient admission data. In *30th Annual International Conference of the IEEE Engineering in Medicine and Biology Society*. Vancouver, 3819–3822.

Boyle, A., Beniuk, K., Higginson, I., Atkinson, P. (2012). Emergency department crowding: Time for interventions and policy evaluations. *Emergency Medicine International.*

Brockwell, P.J., Davis, R.A. (eds). (2002). *Introduction to time series and forecasting.* Springer, Berlin.

Brown, R.G. (1959). *Statistical Forecasting for Inventory Control.* McGraw-Hill, New York.

Bunn, D.W. (1985). Statistical efficiency in the linear combination of forecasts. *International Journal of Forecasting*, 1(2), 151–163.

Champion, R., Kinsman, L.D., Lee, G.A., Masman, K.A., May, E.A., Mills, T.M., Taylor, M.D., Thomas, P.R., Williams, R.J. (2007). Forecasting emergency department presentations. *Australian Health Review: A Publication of the Australian Hospital Association*, 31(1), 83–90.

Chatfield, C. (1993). Calculating interval forecasts. *Journal of Business and Economic Statistics*, 11(2), 121–135.

Chatfield, C. (2016). *The Analysis of Time Series: An Introduction.* CRC Press, Boca Raton.

Clarke, S.M., Griebsch, J.H., Simpson, T.W. (2004). Analysis of support vector regression for approximation of complex engineering analyses. *Journal of Mechanical Design*, 127(6), 1077–1087.

Clemen, R.T. (1989). Combining forecasts: A review and annotated bibliography. *International Journal of Forecasting*, 5(4), 559–583.

Cleveland, R.B., Cleveland, W.S., Terpenning, I. (1990). Stl: A seasonal-trend decomposition procedure based on loess. *Journal of Official Statistics*, 6(1), 3.

Cooke, M., Wilson, S., Halsall, J., Roalfe, A. (2004). Total time in English accident and emergency departments is related to bed occupancy. *Emergency Medicine Journal*, 575–576.

Coskun, N., Erol, R. (2010). An optimization model for locating and sizing emergency medical service stations. *Journal of Medical Systems*, 34(1), 43–49.

Crone, S.F., Hibon, M., Nikolopoulos, K. (2014). Corrigendum to 'Advances in forecasting with neural networks? Empirical evidence from the NN3 competition on time series prediction'. *International Journal of Forecasting*, 30(4), 1138.

Cummins, J.D., Griepentrog, G.L. (1985). Forecasting automobile insurance paid claim costs using econometric and ARIMA models. *International Journal of Forecasting*, 1(3), 203–215.

Derlet, R., Richards, J., Kravitz, R. (2001). Frequent overcrowding in U.S. emergency departments. *Academic Emergency Medicine: Official Journal of the Society for Academic Emergency Medicine*, 8(2), 151–155.

Dhrymes, P.J., Peristiani, S.C. (1988). A comparison of the forecasting performance of WEFA and ARIMA time series methods. *International Journal of Forecasting*, 4(1), 81–101.

Di Caprio, U., Genesio, R., Pozzi, S., Vicino, A. (1983). Short term load forecasting in electric power systems: A comparison of ARMA models and extended wiener filtering. *Journal of Forecasting*, 2(1), 59–76.

Ekström, A., Kurland, L., Farrokhnia, N., Castrén, M., Nordberg, M. (2014). Forecasting emergency department visits using internet data. *Annals of Emergency Medicine*, 65(4), 436–442.

Findley, D.F., Monsell, B.C. (1998). New capabilities and methods of the X-12-ARIMA seasonal-adjustment program. *Journal of Business & Economic Statistics*, 16(2), 127.

Foley, M., Kifaieh, N., Mallon, W.K. (2011). Financial impact of emergency department crowding. *Western Journal of Emergency Medicine*, 12(2), 192–197.

Gendreau, M., Ferland, J., Gendron, B., Hail, N., Jaumard, B., Lapierre, S., Pesant, G., Soriano, P. (2007). Physician scheduling in emergency rooms. In *Practice and Theory of Automated Timetabling VI*, Burke, E.K., Rudová, H. (eds). Springer, Berlin, 53–66.

Geurts, M.D., Kelly, J.P. (1986). Forecasting retail sales using alternative models. *International Journal of Forecasting*, 2(3), 261–272.

Gilson, L. (2003). Trust and the development of health care as a social institution. *Social Science & Medicine*, 56(7), 1453–1468.

de Gooijer, J.G., Hyndman, R.J. (2006). 25 years of time series forecasting. *International Journal of Forecasting*, 22(3), 443–473.

Grambsch, P., Stahel, W.A. (1990). Forecasting demand for special telephone services. *International Journal of Forecasting*, 6(1), 53–64.

Granger, C.W.J., Ramanathan, R. (1984). Improved methods of combining forecasts. *Journal of Forecasting*, 3(2), 197–204.

Gunter, S.I. (1992). Nonnegativity restricted least squares combinations. *International Journal of Forecasting*, 8(1), 45–59.

Han, J.H., Zhou, C., France, D.J., Zhong, S., Jones, I., Storrow, A.B., Aronsky, D. (2007). The effect of emergency department expansion on emergency department overcrowding. *Academic Emergency Medicine: Official Journal of the Society for Academic Emergency Medicine*, 14(4), 338–343.

Hein, S.E., Spudeek, R.E. (1988). Forecasting the daily federal funds rate. *International Journal of Forecasting*, 4(4), 581–591.

Heuts, R.M.J., Bronckers, J.H.J.M. (1988). Forecasting the Dutch heavy truck market. *International Journal of Forecasting*, 4(1), 57–79.

Hibon, M., Evgeniou, T. (2005). To combine or not to combine: Selecting among forecasts and their combinations. *International Journal of Forecasting*, 21(1), 15–24.

Hillmer, S.C., Larcker, D.F., Schroeder, D.A. (1983). Forecasting accounting data: A multiple time-series analysis. *Journal of Forecasting*, 2(4), 389–404.

Hirotugu, A. (1974). A new look at the statistical model identification. *IEEE Transactions on Automatic Control*, 19(6), 716–723.

Holt, C.C. (2004). Forecasting seasonals and trends by exponentially weighted moving averages. *International Journal of Forecasting*, 20(1), 5–10.

Hong, W.C. (2009). Electric load forecasting by support vector model. *Applied Mathematical Modelling*, 33(5), 2444–2454.

Hyndman, R.J., Koelher, A.B., Snyder, R.D., Grose, S. (2002). A state space framework for automatic forecasting using exponential smoothing methods. *International Journal of Forecasting*, 18(3), 439–454.

Jalalpour, M., Gel, Y., Levin, S. (2015). Forecasting demand for health services: Development of a publicly available toolbox. *Operations Research for Health Care*, 5, 1–9.

Jones, S.A., Joy, M.P., Pearson, J. (2002). Forecasting demand of emergency care. *Health Care Management Science*, 5(4), 297–305.

Jones, S.S., Evans, R.S., Allen, T.L., Thomas, A., Haug, P.J., Welch, S.J., Snow, G.L. (2009). A multivariate time series approach to modeling and forecasting demand in the emergency department. *Journal of Biomedical Informatics*, 42(1), 123–139.

Kadri, F., Harrou, F., Chaabane, S., Tahon, C. (2014). Time series modeling and forecasting of emergency department overcrowding. *Journal of Medical Systems*, 38(9), 1–20.

Kutty, V.R. (2000). Historical analysis of the development of health care facilities in Kerala State, India. *Health Policy and Planning*, 15(1), 103–109.

Lam, J.C., Wan, K.K.W., Liu, D., Tsang, C.L. (2010). Multiple regression models for energy use in air-conditioned office buildings in different climates. *Energy Conversion and Management*, 51(12), 2692–2697.

Layton, A.P., Defris, L.V., Zehnwirth, B. (1986). An international comparison of economic leading indicators of telecommunications traffic. *International Journal of Forecasting*, 2(4), 413–425.

Lin, W.T. (1989). Modeling and forecasting hospital patient movements: Univariate and multiple time series approaches. *International Journal of Forecasting*, 5(2), 195–208.

Lin, B.Y-J., Hsu Cliff, C.P., Chao, M-C., Luh, S.-P., Hung, S.-W., Breen, G.M. (2008). Physician and nurse job climates in hospital-based emergency departments in Taiwan: Management and implications. *Journal of Medical Systems*, 32(4), 269–281.

Luo, L., Luo, Y., You, Y., Cheng, Y., Shi, Y., Gong, R. (2016). A MIP model for rolling horizon surgery scheduling. *Journal of Medical Systems*, 40(5), 127.

Medina, D.C., Findley, S.E., Guindo, B., Doumbia, S. (2007). Forecasting non-stationary diarrhea, acute respiratory infection, and malaria time-series in Niono, Mali. *PLoS ONE*, 2(11).

de Menezes, L.M., Bunn, D.W. (1998). The persistence of specification problems in the distribution of combined forecast errors. *International Journal of Forecasting*, 14(3), 415–426.

Mielczarek, B. (2013). Estimating future demand for hospital emergency services at the regional level. In *Simulation Conference (WSC), 2013 Winter*. Washington, 2386–2397.

Miller, C.M., Clemen, R.T., Winkler, R.L. (1992). The effect of nonstationarity on combined forecasts. *International Journal of Forecasting*, 7(4), 515–529.

Milner, P.C. (1988). Forecasting the demand on accident and emergency departments in health districts in the Trent region. *Statistics in Medicine*, 7(10), 1061–1072.

Newbold, P., Granger, C.W.J. (1974). Experience with forecasting univariate time series and combination of forecasts. *Journal of the Royal Statistical Society. Series A*. 137(2), 131–165.

Panorama Urgences (2013). Est-RESCUE [Online]. Available at: https:// www.est-rescue.fr/ [Accessed 3 January].

Pflaumer, P. (1992). Forecasting US population totals with the Box-Jenkins approach. *International Journal of Forecasting*, 8(3), 329–338.

du Preez, J., Witt, S.F. (2003). Univariate versus multivariate time series forecasting: An application to international tourism demand. *International Journal of Forecasting*, 19(3), 435–451.

Sanders, N.R. (2001). Forecasting theory. In *Wiley Encyclopedia of Electrical and Electronics Engineering*. John Wiley & Sons, New York.

Schull, M.J., Mamdani, M.M., Fang, J. (2005). Influenza and emergency department utilization by elders. *Academic Emergency Medicine: Official Journal of the Society for Academic Emergency Medicine*, 12(4), 338–344.

Shahrabi, J., Hadavandi, E., Asadi, S. (2013). Developing a hybrid intelligent model for forecasting problems: Case study of tourism demand time series. *Knowledge-Based Systems*, 43, 112–122.

Shi, H.-J., Tsai, J.-T., Ho, W.H., Lee, K.-T. (2011). Autoregressive integrated moving average model for long-term prediction of emergency department revenue and visitor volume. In *2011 International Conference on Machine Learning and Cybernetics*. Guilin, 979–982.

Stout, J.W.A., Tawney, B. (2005). An Excel forecasting model to aid in decision-making that affects hospital resource/bed utilization – Hospital capability to admit emergency room patients. In *2005 IEEE Systems and Information Engineering Design Symposium*. University of Virginia, Charlottesville, 222–228.

Sun, Y., Heng, B.H., Seow, Y.T., Seow, E. (2009). Forecasting daily attendances at an emergency department to aid resource planning. *BMC Emergency Medicine*, 9(1), 1–9.

Sun, B.C., Hsia, R.Y., Weiss, R.E., Zingmond, D., Liang, J.L., Han, W., McCreath, H., Asch, S.A. (2013). Effect of emergency department crowding on outcomes of admitted patients. *Annals of Emergency Medicine*, 61(6), 605–611.

Taylor, J.W., Bunn, D.W. (1999). Investigating improvements in the accuracy of prediction intervals for combinations of forecasts: A simulation study. *International Journal of Forecasting*, 15(3), 325–339.

Tso, G.K.F., Yau, K.K.W. (2007). Predicting electricity energy consumption: A comparison of regression analysis, decision tree and neural networks. *Energy*, 32(9), 1761–1768.

Walker, G. (1931). On periodicity in series of related terms. *Proceedings of the Royal Society of London A: Mathematical, Physical and Engineering Sciences*, 131(818), 518–532.

Winkler, R.L., Makridakis, S. (1983). The combination of forecasts. *Journal of the Royal Statistical Society, Series A*, 146(2), 150–157.

Winters, P.R. (1960). Forecasting sales by exponentially weighted moving averages. *Management Science*, 6(3), 324–342.

Yalaoui, A., Chehade, H., Yalaoui, F., Amodeo, L. (2012). *Optimization of Logistics*. ISTE Ltd London and John Wiley & Sons, New York.

Yang, L., Lam, J.C., Liu, J., Tsang, C.L. (2008). Building energy simulation using multi-years and typical meteorological years in different climates. *Energy Conversion and Management*, 49(1), 113–124.

Yu, D., Blocker, R.C., Sir, M.Y., Hallbeck, M.S., Hellmich, T.R., Cohen, T., Nestler, D.M., Pasupathy, K.S. (2016). Intelligent emergency department: Validation of sociometers to study workload. *Journal of Medical Systems*, 40(3), 53.

Yule, G.U. (1927). On a method of investigating periodicities in disturbed series, with special reference to Wolfer's sunspot numbers. *Philosophical Transactions of the Royal Society of London A: Mathematical, Physical and Engineering Sciences*, 226(636–646), 267–298.

6

Positioning and Innovations from the Champagne Sud Hospitals in the World of Hospital Logistics

6.1. Introduction

The hospital logistics commission of the ASLOG (*Association française pour la logistique*, French Logistics Association) defines hospital logistics as "the management of the flow of patients, products, materials, services and information relating to them in order to ensure that quality and safety meet a defined standard of performance and efficiency, from the supplier to the patient and, depending on the case, the final user". Hospital logistics, therefore, is a field of study and optimization of two types of physical hospital flows: the flow of people (which consists of the movements of patients from their arrival until they leave the establishment, as well as the staff and visitors) and the flow of material. This material is very varied and is at the center of a care unit with incoming flows as follows: patient files, labile blood products, medication, sterile and non-sterile medical equipment, meals, clean linen, general consumables, mail and parcels. The outgoing flows are as follows: samples, equipment to be sterilized, used cutlery, crockery and linen, waste, mail and parcels.

Chapter written by Moïse NOUMBISSI TCHOUPO, Alice YALAOUI, Lionel AMODEO and Farouk YALAOUI.

Around the world, the hospital world comes up against scaling and organization challenges in order to satisfy patient needs. These needs may often be urgent and require high quality and safety. In this context, we find complex systems, which are increasingly being studied by operational research, with the aim of bringing in optimized solutions while respecting a pre-established set of rules.

From 1980 to 2001, research conducted on the evaluation of logistics activity in the hospital world estimated that in France, this total represents approximately 31–34% of a hospital's activity (Bourgeon *et al.* 2001; Henning 1980; Kowalski 1991). Other, more recent, studies have concluded that it would be possible to reduce costs associated with hospital logistics by 15% (Davis 2004). From these studies, we can conclude that hospital logistics are a crucial area for economizing in hospitals and that this would require reorganization and the implementation of smarter systems.

The Champagne Sud hospitals are currently carrying out a review to improve the management of processes and procedures within their logistics network. This is being done through smart digitization, brought about through techniques tried and tested through operational research. However, the hospital has also clearly demonstrated its ambition of bringing about innovations in techniques by funding studies and the creation of tools. This is the framework within which our project has taken place. Within the framework of a CIFRE study[1], a collaborative project between the University of Technology of Troyes and the Troyes hospital center (THC), we work on optimizing logistics in the case of the flow of materials. These studies are part of a CIFRE project in partnership with THC.

THC is the largest employer in Aube, with an operating budget of 232.4 million euros, including 11.2 million euros of investment. It is made up of:

– the Hauts-Clos hospital;

– the Comte Henri residence;

– the retirement home in the Nazareth estate.

---

1 Industrial agreements for training through research, a program that funds companies that take in a doctoral student who is at the center of a collaborative project between the company and a public laboratory.

In France, the application of operational research has made contributions at all levels of decision making (strategic, tactical and operational). The resources made available and the time necessary to bring about solutions to such complex problems are calculated over a period of months. However, as we will see in this chapter, operational research with much lower resources allows us to propose solutions in terms of minutes or even seconds.

In the University of Tours, the doctoral work of Kergosien *et al.* (2011) was carried out in collaboration with the François Rabelais University of Tours focused on the problem of the transport of product flows and patient flows (allocation of transport to patients in real time through ambulances). To resolve the problems faced in this field, several methods inspired by operational research techniques were proposed: exact methods (linear programming models with whole numbers) and heuristic methods (greedy algorithms, tabu search with and without adaptive memory, genetic algorithms, mimetic algorithms). In the context of this project, the underlying problem of pickup and delivery was framed in a very specific way: indeed, the journeys made by vehicles are either for delivery or for pickup. Further, changing a vehicle is not allowed, which leaves scope for improvement in the quality of the solutions put in place. In fact, changing vehicles would make it possible to increase the utilization rate for the vehicles and thus maintain a fleet of optimal size.

In 2011, Virginie (André 2011) worked on the organization of flows of different products circulating in a hospital. There is a partnership between the Clermont-Ferrand teaching hospital and partner universities, such as the LIMOS research laboratory (*laboratoire d'informatique en modélisation et optimisation des systèmes*, Laboratory of Information Sciences for Modeling and Optimizing Systems) in Clermont-Ferrand. This partnership also enabled the study of other problems such as the scheduling of the surgical unit and the optimization of the medication circuit. Another example of a study that highlighted the scientific aspect of the problem of pickup and delivery, with considerations closer to reality, is the study carried out by Xu *et al.* (2003). However, this study worked on the fixed rule that "the delivery demands must be carried out in reverse order compared to the corresponding pickup demands".

Our studies follow these studies, while considering aspects that these studies did not approach. In our case study, we take into account the journeys made by good drivers and also consider the welfare of the drivers on these journeys. This involves ensuring that rules regarding working hours, driving hours and rest times are respected. Thus, in our construction of the journeys, we work on the general case, without restricting ourselves to the problem of pickup or delivery. In other words, the only restriction we have taken into account is that it is not possible to deliver something that was not first collected. To the best of our knowledge, this problem has not been approached in previous studies. Further, in practice, the different flows (meals, linen, pharmacy, etc.) are transported in trolleys of different dimensions (length, width and height) in trucks that are also of different dimensions. This aspect, which has not been approached in literature so far, has been integrated into our work.

The NP-hard nature has already been demonstrated for the subproblems of the problem that we are working on. Indeed, earlier studies have demonstrated the level of difficulty of the problem of pickup and delivery within specific time windows (Dumas *et al.* 1991; Cordeau and Laporte 2003). To propose an efficient method for solving this problem, we have first worked on a tiered approach to the problem. At every step, this gave us proven methods to build on further. Our solutions at each step have been tested against instances in literature (when the problem was not new) or against instances taken from the THC's daily experiences. As we will see further on, the approaches we developed are efficient, not only in terms of the quality of the solution but also in terms of the computation time.

In the following sections, we will discuss hospital logistics and the links it has with operational research. We will then present the approach that we propose to solve this problem. Finally, we will present some optimization methods and techniques that we proposed and tested on real-life instances, as well as those taken from literature. These techniques focus on the problem of optimizing the journeys made by the vehicle for pickups and deliveries, while respecting the time windows for each visit and the capacity of the vehicle being used.

6.2. The hospital logistics problem

According to (Chow *et al.* 1994), hospital logistics activities can be divided into three categories:

– supplies: the process of buying and managing stocks of different products;

– production: transformative processes such as the washing of linen, the preparation of meals or the sterilization of equipment;

– distribution (or resupplying): the transport of transformed products in containers from the production units to the storage areas, before being used for patients.

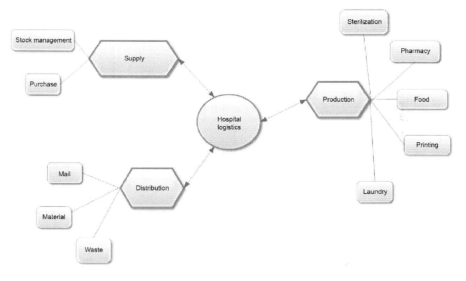

Figure 6.1. *The different logistics functions, from Chow et al. (1994)*

To the logistics functions given in Figure 6.1, we can also add the components of distribution: the distribution of food, laundry and pharmaceutical products flows.

6.2.1. *Operational research and the hospital world*

There are diverse applications of techniques developed in operational research in the hospital world. For a comprehensive view of this field, there are several general state-of-the-art discussions. One of the first studies to approach this problem was by Fries (1976); we then had projects proposed by researchers (Boldy 1987; Boldy and O'Kane 1982; Rosenhead 1978; Wiers 1997), who carried out literature reviews and offered propositions for classifying problems encountered in the hospital world and that had been studied through operational research. There are also other reviews dedicated to recurrent problems in the hospital world, such as the organization of the surgical units (Cardoen *et al.* 2010), planning working hours for nurses (Burke *et al.* 2004), the criteria for measuring the performance of a health system (Li and Benton 1996), or the process of hierarchical analysis for decision-making in the medical field (Liberatore and Nydick 2008). More recently, (Castillo-Salazar *et al.* 2016) proposed a literature review on the subject of planning patient transport. The problems tackled by operational reviews are related to the patient's pathway from the time they are taken into care in their residence (ambulance journeys) to their discharge and return to their residence, with, in between, the care administered in emergency services, putting in place care teams, and organizing medication, meals and clean linen. All these components that contribute to the patient care and to the patient's well-being are brought in so they may be ready at the right time and the right place: techniques for planning under constraint, sequencing, journeys made by vehicles and stock management.

Table 6.1 lists the most recent work on problems of pickup and delivery in a fixed time frame and with a heterogeneous fleet of vehicles. It can be seen that no study on pickup and delivery studies the size of the fleet.

6.2.2. *Description, formalization and solution approach*

The goal of the research carried out in the context of optimizing logistics within the THC was to propose an efficient solution in order to re-size the team of drivers and the fleet of trucks. The chosen time horizons for planning was a weekly timeframe, as the requirements are periodical on a weekly basis. The costs we retained for our study are:

– the cost incurred by the number of drivers;

– the fixed cost incurred by the acquisition of the fleet of vehicles;

– the fuel costs used to cover all requirements.

The scaling of the team of drivers is subject to regulations on driving time and the break time for drivers operating vehicles larger than 3.5T and the regulations on working hours for an employee of a public hospital in France. When setting up the timetable for a driver, it may be that the driver changes vehicles and, in this case, the changeover time must also be considered.

Characteristics	Publications	(Noumbissi Tchoupo et al. 2016)	(Dumas et al. 1991)	(Xu et al. 2003)	(Qu and Bard 2013)	(Betinelli et al. 2014)	(Irnich 2000)
Contexts	Vehicle with an adjustable capacity				X		
	Heterogeneous fleet of vehicles	X	X	X		X	X
	Scaling the fleet of vehicles				X		
	Different types of products			X			
	Possibility of overshooting the time window					X	
	Multiple windows			X			
Constraints	Parity constraints	X	X	X	X	X	X
	Respecting the transit window	X	X	X	X	X	
	Constraints around capacity of the vehicle	X	X	X		X	
	Constraints regarding precedence between a pickup request and an associated delivery request	X	X	X	X	X	X
	Duration of the journey			X			
Performance indicators	Fixed cost of the vehicles	X			X		
	Fuel costs	X	X	X	X	X	X
	Cost of not adhering to the timeframe					X	
	Time spent in the vehicle				X		
Resolution methods	Branch and price method					X	
	Column generation method		X	X			
	Benders' decomposition method	X					
	Two phase heuristics				X		

Table 6.1. *Pickup and delivery problems with a heterogeneous fleet of vehicles*

Publications	Problems	Characteristics	Objectives	Types of products
(Kergosien et al. *2013)*	Transport of products between hospitals; scaling teams	Meta heuristics, genetic algorithm (Mitchell *et al.* 1996) and tabu search (Glover 1989)	Minimizing the sum of the hours of the arrivals and the number of employees required	Pharmaceutical consumables
(Medaglia et al. *2009)*	Search for the best site to process hospital waste	Problem with dual goals of positioning the installations (MIP), heuristics	Multiple-objectives: minimizing the transport costs, minimizing the number of employees assigned	Waste
(Shih and Chang 2001)	Planning of routes for periodic collection of waste in a logistics network	PVRP and MIP to assign routes for days of the week	Minimizing the transport costs, minimizing the number of kilometers traveled on a daily basis	Waste
(Swaminathan 2003)	Allocation of rare medicines to hospitals	Resolved with a heuristic	Minimizing the total value of the budget for medicines, leave/maximize the total value of the budget allocated for medications	Pharmaceutical products
Studied problem	Designing transport flows between hospitals and suppliers; scaling the team of drivers; scaling the fleet of vehicles	Linear program, ant colony algorithm	Minimizing the total cost (cost of the number of drivers used, fixed cost of the use of vehicles and the total fuel costs)	Linen, medication, meals and shop products

Table 6.2. *Publications on the problems of external hospital logistics coupled with the problem of assigning drivers (Volland et al. 2017)*

A requirement (or request) is defined as a request for collecting a quantity (number of trolleys) of a type of product from one site and a request for delivery of whatever has been collected to another site. Each request is characterized by the data: regarding the product type, a trolley number for this product type, a timeframe within which this operation must be carried out and the duration required for the operation to be carried out (loading, unloading and cleaning the vehicle). Each request is fulfilled by a driver by carrying out the pickup request before the associated delivery request using the same vehicle. In our case study, there are two types of flows: the supply flow and the removal flow. The supply flow corresponds to the pickup from the suppliers for delivery to the care service. The removal flow corresponds to pickup from the care service for delivery to the processing centers. The removal flow for meals or linen involves collecting meal trolleys or used linen trolleys that are sent to the central kitchen or the laundry, respectively. For medicines (or equipment), this involves returning empty trolleys to be used again for future deliveries.

Each type of product (food, linen, medicine and equipment) is delivered in a specific type of trolley. Consequently, four types of trolleys are considered and each has specific dimensions. The trolleys cannot be piled one atop the other, thus the chosen dimensions for the trolleys are length and width. The fact that the products are transported on trolleys poses the problem of arranging this across two dimensions during each pickup round in order to respect the constraints regarding the capacity of the truck. Our case study also presents constraints related to compatibility:

– product/product compatibility (certain products cannot be transported together);

– product/truck compatibility (certain products must be transported in specific vehicles, and this is the case with meal trolleys, for example, which must be transported in refrigerated trucks to conserve the cold chain);

– truck/request site compatibility (certain requests emanate from sites with specific access constraints).

Figure 6.2 presents an example of a solution to a problem consisting of five requests (hence, 10 requirements: five pickups and five deliveries), three vehicles and five types of flow (clean linen, used linen, equipment, meals and medication) The proposed solution consists of two drivers using three trucks and the objective is to satisfy all demands. Each request made up of a pickup/delivery pair is carried out by the same driver and the same truck. Further, each pickup is made before its corresponding delivery. It is assumed that constraints relating to the time frame, capacity, compatibility and various regulations are respected. The first driver uses only one kind of vehicle and the second driver changes vehicles during his break.

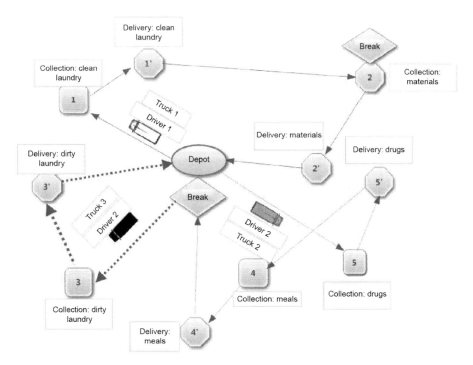

Figure 6.2. *Example of a problem*

The problem approached here is difficult as it is an extension of problem of pickup and delivery within a time frame, which is an NP-hard problem (Xu *et al.* 2003). In literature, research has been carried out on problems close to the one we pose (André 2011; Kergosien *et al.* 2011; Xu *et al.* 2003). However, these studies have not simultaneously considered all the aspects of the problem explored in our study. To propose efficient algorithms to resolve this problem, rich in the diversity of the problems that constitute it, we present a sequential resolution approach in order to use the different solutions proposed to resolve the subproblems.

6.3. Innovative methods and techniques

In this section, we propose a hierarchization of the problem in order to construct a complete solution to it using the solutions to the subproblems. We will also discuss some methods that we proposed and which were proven to be effective regarding the subproblem of journeys made by vehicle. In this section, since the research has not yet been published, we will not discuss the approaches that lead to a solution which integrate other tiers apart from that of vehicle journeys.

We proposed a hierarchization into four steps:

1) proposing a solution method to the pickup and delivery problem with a given time frame;

2) integrating the problems of compatibility between flows, between trucks and the flow being transported, and between trucks and the delivery or pickup site;

3) integrating the multiple dimension aspect (two dimensions) of the capacity of the vehicles, as the flows are transported in specific trolleys, in trucks whose containers are of different sizes;

4) integrating rules on breaks, rest time and driving time for the drivers.

The proposed approach is presented diagrammatically in Figure 6.3. This approach made it possible to carry out reorganization in 6 months, with considerable gains in the order of 10.8% (tens of thousands of euros/year). Further, we observed a decrease of over 71% (hundreds of hours per year) in waiting time before the requests were taken up by drivers.

In the following sections, we present the different work we carried out in order to integrate the subproblems and we propose a comprehensive solution method to the problem.

6.3.1. *The problem of pickups and deliveries within a time frame and with a homogeneous fleet of vehicles*

Several recent studies have explored the problem of pickups and deliveries with using a homogeneous fleet. For one of the definitions of this problem, see the article by Dumas *et al.* (1991). In this variant, we proposed an efficient meta-heuristic, which is a hybridization of the ant colony algorithm with dedicated local search algorithms. We chose the ant colony algorithm because it constructed actionable solutions, unlike some other algorithms (for instance, the genetic algorithm), which often require a reconstruction in order to obtain actionable solutions.

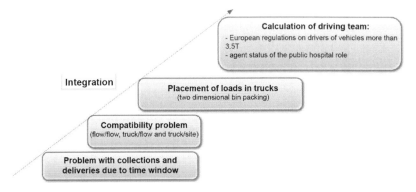

Figure 6.3. *Approach to the solution*

The heuristics for the ant colony were first proposed by Dorigo and Gambardella (1997) for research on the optimal pathways in a graph. It was inspired by the work of Goss *et al.* (1989), who studied the behavior of ants finding a path between their colonies and a food source. This technique led to several successes when used with combinatorial optimization problems. This was the case with the research carried out by Belmecheri *et al.* (2009) to resolve a problem with vehicular journeys within a certain time frame and using a heterogeneous fleet of vehicles.

An ant constructs a solution made up of a set of routes and each route is traveled by a vehicle. The routes are constructed in a sequential manner. A new route is added if all the demands are not satisfied and no routes can be inserted into the route under construction. Local searches have been proposed for each aspect of the goal to be achieved:

– reducing the cost of each route constructed (H1 algorithms);

– reducing the total cost of a solution due to the number of vehicles (H2 algorithms);

– reducing the fuel consumption in a solution (H3 algorithms).

The pseudopod of the proposed algorithm is given by:

Constructing an initial solution
while *the best solution is not improved after a given number of iterations* **do**
    for *each ant in the population* **do**
        Construct a new solution that satisfies all demands
        while *we can delete one route* **do**
           | Applying, respectively, the algorithms H2, H1 and H3
        end
        if *The current solution has the same number of vehicles as the best solution that was found* **then**
           while *the total distance decreases* **do**
              | Applying, respectively, the algorithms: H2 and H3
           end
        end
        Carrying out a local update of the pheromones
    end
    Carrying out an overall update of the pheromones
end

Algorithm 6.1. *Pseudopod for the ACO hybrid*

For more details on this solution method, see (Noumbissi Tchoupo *et al.* 2017).

The experimental results for 56 instances of 100 requests in *Benchmark* by Li and Lim (2003) showed that the proposed hybrid meta-heuristic is better than existing algorithms, up to then, to resolve this kind of a problem. Indeed, in 98.2% (55/56) of the cases, a best solution or a solution equal to the best-known solution was found and it found a better solution than the best-known solution in 44.6% (25/56) of cases.

6.3.2. *Pickup and delivery problems with a time frame and a heterogeneous fleet of vehicles of finite size*

Work carried out on the $P2$ problem (Noumbissi Tchoupo *et al.* 2016) made it possible to determine efficient techniques to reduce the search space for solutions. Valid inequalities were proposed for this problem. This problem was modeled by generalizing the formulation proposed by Grandinetti *et al.* (2014) for the case of a homogeneous fleet of vehicles. And to solve this problem we proposed an algorithm based on Benders decomposition.

In the following section, we will consider a heterogeneous fleet of vehicles K. Each vehicle, k, with a capacity Q^k, a fixed cost δ^k and a cost v^k per kilometer traveled. Each vehicle's journey begins and ends at the depot. Let n be the number of requests. Each request consists of a pair: a pickup request and a delivery request. All requests must be satisfied. Let A be the set of arcs and V be the set of vertices. The graph for the transports is modeled by a direct graph $G =< V, A >$, where $V = \{0, 1, \cdots, n, n+1, \cdots, 2n, 2n+1\}$. The vertices 0 and $2n+1$ are the fictional requests modeling the departure from and return to the depot. An arc $(i, j) \in A$ if $max\{t_{0i}, a_i\} + s_i + t_{ij} \leq b_j$ and $i \neq j$. Let $P \subset V$ designate the subset of vertices representing the set of pickup requests and $D \subset V$ the set of delivery requests. For any request $i \in P$, $q_i > 0$ represents the quantity to be collected and for any request $i \in D$, $q_i < 0$ is the quantity to be delivered. The negativity of the quantities for the delivery requests is due to the fact that they correspond to a reduction in the number of trolleys present in the vehicle after a delivery request has been carried out. Each request $i \in V$ corresponds to a window for the visit $[a_i, b_i]$. For all $i \in P$, $n+i$ designates the associated delivery request and $|q_i| = |q_{n+i}|$. t_{ij} is the Euclidian distance between the requesting sites i and j, and s_i is the time required to carry out the service i. In practice, s_i is the time required for loading or unloading the request i and does not depend only on the number of trolleys but also on the characteristics of the site.

The variables in the decision are: $x_{i,j}^k$, which is a binary variable whose value is 1 if the vehicle k satisfies the demand i and then j, 0 if not; B_i^k, which is the continuous variable representing the date of commencement of the servicing of the request i by the vehicle k; $Q_{i,j}^k$, which represents the number of trolleys present in the vehicle k on the arc (i, j). For the next part, let us write:

$$c_{i,j}^k = v^k d_{ij} \qquad [6.1]$$

n	Number of requests
A	Set of arcs
V	Set of vertices (requests)
P	Set of pickup requests
D	Set of delivery requests
K	Set of vehicles
Q^k	Capacity of the vehicle k
δ^k	Fixed cost of the vehicle k
v^k	Cost per kilometer for the vehicle k
$|q_i|$	Quantity of i to be delivered or collected
a_i	Earliest start date for i
b_i	Latest start date for i
s_i	Service time for i
$t_{i,j}$	Journey time from i to j
$d_{i,j}$	Distance traveled from i to j
$n+i$	Delivery corresponding to the pickup i

Table 6.3. *Notations*

This is written in a linear mathematical program with mixed numbers as:

$$Min \sum_{i \in P} \sum_{k \in K} \delta_k x_{0i}^k + \sum_{(i,j) \in A} \sum_{k \in K} c_{ij}^k x_{ij}^k \qquad [6.2]$$

$$\forall i \in P, \ \sum_{k \in K} \sum_{(i,j) \in A} x_{ij}^k = 1 \qquad [6.3]$$

$$\forall (i,k) \in P \times K, \ \sum_{j|(i,j) \in A} x_{ij}^k = \sum_{j|(n+i,j) \in A} x_{n+ij} \qquad [6.4]$$

$$\forall k \in K, \ \sum_{i \in P} x_{0i}^k \leq 1 \qquad [6.5]$$

$$\forall k \in K, \ \sum_{i \in P} x_{0i}^k = \sum_{i \in D} x_{i(2n+1)}^k \qquad [6.6]$$

$$\forall (i,k) \in P \cup D \times K, \ \sum_{j|(i,j) \in A} x_{ij}^k \leq \sum_{j \in P} x_{0j}^k \qquad [6.7]$$

$$\forall (i,k) \in P \cup D \times K \qquad\qquad\qquad\qquad\qquad\qquad\qquad [6.8]$$

$$\sum_{j|(i,j)\in A} x_{ij}^k - \sum_{j|(j,i)\in A} x_{ji}^k = 0 \qquad\qquad\qquad\qquad\qquad [6.9]$$

$$\forall (i,j) \in A, \forall k \in K, \quad B_i^k - b_i + (b_i + s_i + t_{ij})x_{ij}^k \le B_j^k \qquad [6.10]$$

$$\forall (i,k) \in P \times K, \quad B_i^k - B_{n+i}^k + (s_i + t_{in+i})\sum_{j \in V} x_{ij}^k \le 0 \qquad [6.11]$$

$$\forall (i,k) \in V \times K, \quad a_i \sum_{j|(i,j)\in A} x_{ij}^k \le B_i^k \le b_i \sum_{j|(ij)\in A} x_{ij}^k \qquad [6.12]$$

$$\sum_{i \in P}\sum_{k \in K} Q_{0i}^k + \sum_{i \in D}\sum_{k \in K} Q_{i(2n+1)}^k = 0 \qquad\qquad\qquad [6.13]$$

$$\forall i \in N, \quad \sum_{k \in K}\sum_{j|(i,j)\in A} Q_{ij}^k - \sum_{k \in K}\sum_{j|(j,i)\in A} Q_{ji}^k = q_i \qquad [6.14]$$

$$\forall (i,j) \in A, \forall k \in K, \quad Q_{ij}^k \le Q_k x_{ij}^k \qquad\qquad\qquad\qquad [6.15]$$

$$\forall (i,j) \in A, \forall k \in K, \quad x_{ij}^k \in \{0,1\}, \; Q_{ij}^k > 0 \qquad\qquad [6.16]$$

$$\forall (i,k) \in P \times K, \quad B_i^k > 0 \qquad\qquad\qquad\qquad\qquad [6.17]$$

The objective [6.2] is the minimization of the fixed cost of use of the vehicles and the per kilometer cost of the journeys. The constraints [6.3] and [6.4] model the adherence to the time frame and the precedence in service between a pickup point and the corresponding delivery point. Constraint [6.5] obliges vehicles to leave the depot once at most, while constraint [6.6] ensures their return to the depot. Constraint [6.7] obliges the vehicles to leave the depot to service a request. Constraints [6.8], [6.9], [6.10] and [6.11] model the loading of the vehicles along the journey and ensure that the capacity of each vehicle is not violated. Constraint [6.12] ensures that all vehicles leave and return to the depot empty. Constraints [6.13] and [6.14] model the loading of the vehicles along the journey and ensure that the number of trolleys present in each vehicle does not exceed the capacity.

6.3.2.1. *Some techniques to accelerate the solution*

To accelerate the procedure for solving problems in operational research, it is often usual to determine techniques to reduce the solution space before starting on the solution, strictly speaking, of the problem. Based on earlier work, we have proposed results that allow us to reduce the solution space.

Proposed for the first time by Desrochers and Laporte (1991) for TSP with a time frame, (Cordeau 2006) proposed the reinforcement of the limits of the variable B_i by:

$$B_i \geq a_i + \sum_{j \in N \setminus \{i\}} max\{0, a_j - a_i + s_j + t_{ij}\}x_{ij}$$

$$B_i \leq b_i - \sum_{j \in N \setminus \{i\}} max\{0, b_i - b_j + s_i + t_{ij}\}x_{ij}$$

We extend this proposition to the case of a heterogeneous fleet of vehicles through:

$$B_i^k \geq a_i + \sum_{j \in N \setminus \{i\}} max\{0, a_j - a_i + s_j + t_{ij}\}x_{ij}^k, \ \forall k \in K$$

$$B_i^k \leq b_i - \sum_{j \in N \setminus \{i\}} max\{0, b_i - b_j + s_i + t_{ij}\}x_{ij}^k, \ \forall k \in K$$

Let us assume that $Q^0 \leq Q_1 \leq \ldots \leq Q^{|K|}$. We can then see that:

– $(0, n + i)$ is unfeasible $\forall i \in P$;

– $(i, 2n + 1)$ is unfeasible $\forall i \in P$.

For the VRPPDTW problem, $\forall i, j \in P$, Dumas *et al.* (1991) proposed eliminating the arcs:

– $(i, n + j)$, if the route $(j, i, n + j, n + i)$ is unfeasible;

– $(n + i, j)$, if the route $(i, n + i, j, n + j)$ is unfeasible;

– (i, j), if the routes $(i, j, n + i, n + j)$ and $(i, j, n + j, n + i)$ are unfeasible;

– $(n + i, n + j)$, if the routes $(i, j, n + i, n + j)$ and $(j, i, n + i, n + j)$ are unfeasible.

We propose adding:

– (i, i) is unfeasible $\forall i \in N$;

– (i, j) and $(j, n+i)$, are unfeasible, if $a_i + t_{ij} + t_{j,n+i} > b_{n+i} \, \forall i \in P, j \in N \setminus \{0, i, n+i, 2n+1\}$;

– (i, j) is unfeasible, if $q_i + q_j > Q^{|K|} \, \forall i, j \in P$.

6.3.2.2. *Benders' decomposition*

We propose resolving HVRPPDTW by using algorithms based on Benders' decomposition by decomposing the mixed variable linear program (PL). Benders' decomposition is a decomposition method that is used in operational research to resolve linear optimization problems that have a block structure. It is based on the principle of generating constraints as it progresses toward the solution. Proceeding through generation of lines, it may be perceived as the pair to the (Dantzig and Wolfe 1960) decomposition method based on the generation of columns.

The master program, still called the restricted linear program, is given by:

$$(Q) \quad min \sum_{i \in P} \sum_{k \in K} \delta^k x_{0i}^k + \sum_{(i,j) \in A} \sum_{k \in K} c_{ij}^k x_{ij}^k$$

subject to [6.2], [6.12], [6.16] and [6.17].

From now on, an optimal solution of (Q) will be denoted by x^*.

The idea in algorithm 6.2 is to not simultaneously consider the large number of constraints. The advantage that this method offers arises from the fact that it captures a part of the information on the restrictions around precedence in the graph using the results presented in section 6.3.2.1. The number of arcs in the graph is thus reduced and it then appears natural to generate, as we progress, the constraints for the precedences that have been violated.

The impact study on the reduction of the search space, in addition with valid inequalities, shows the efficiency of these techniques in reducing the computation time. Further, we have tested our algorithm on instances from literature (in the case of the fleet of homogeneous vehicles) and obtained optimal solutions for certain instances.

1) Solve (Q);
if x^* *is feasible* **then**
| 2) x^* is optimal for (PL), stop.
else
| **while** *there exists a constraint capacity violated by* x^* **do**
| 3) Adding in Q the violated constraints ;
| 4) Solving (Q);
| **end**
| x^* is an optimal solution for (PL), stop.
end

Algorithm 6.2. *Algorithm*

The logistics center of the THC includes a fleet of vehicles of different capacities. The pickup and delivery requests are periodic, over a period of 7 days and thus, we have seven instances, one per day. Using instances from the THC, the algorithm for the Benders' decomposition optimally solved all the instances (one instance/day), with a mean computation time of 10 min.

6.3.3. *Pickup and delivery problem with a time frame and a heterogeneous fleet of vehicles of infinite size*

In this section, we present the work we did on the new problem that we introduced and that was born out of a real-life problem. To the best of our knowledge, this problem has never been studied in literature and so we proposed a new set of instances that came out of the coupling of the instances from Li and Lim (for requests) and Liu and Shen (1999) for the different types of vehicles.

We propose a column-generation algorithm in which the subproblem of finding the variable for the negative reduced cost is subdivided into subproblems (a problem for each vehicle type). The type of subproblem has been identified as a restricted shortest route denoted by *ESPPTWCPD* (*Elementary Shortest Path Problem with Time Windows, Capacity, and Pickup and Delivery*).

Linear models with whole numbers have been proposed to model and resolve the subproblems. To accelerate the solution of the subproblems, certain heuristics have been proposed.

6.3.3.1. *Modeling*

In this section, we model the problem of pickups and deliveries using a heterogeneous fleet as a problem of partitioning of demands. Each partition is a route traveled by one type of vehicle. A route starts at ends at the depot, 0, while satisfying a series of requests and respecting the constraints of the time windows, the capacity of the vehicles and the constraints related to the coupling of the demands. The coupling constraints express the fact that any pickup request is coupled with a delivery request, such that the requests for pickup and delivery are carried out in the same journey and the pickup request must be satisfied before the associated delivery request.

Let K be the set of the types of vehicles. Let $\mathcal{R}^k$ denote the set of feasible routes for a type of vehicle $k \in K$ and let us posit $\mathcal{R} = \bigcup_{k \in K} \mathcal{R}^k$.

For each route $r \in \mathcal{R}^k$, the fuel cost is denoted by c_r^k. Let $\mathcal{R}_r^k$ be the subset of requests fulfilled by the route $r \in \mathcal{R}^k$. Let λ_s be a binary variable equal to 1 if the route $s \in \mathcal{R}$ is integrated into the solution and 0, if not. We can see that for all $s \in \mathcal{R}$, there exist a $k_s \in K$ and $r_s \in \mathcal{R}^{k_s}$ such that: $s = r_s$. We model the problem through:

$$(MP) \quad Min \quad \sum_{s \in \mathcal{R}} (f^{k_s} + c_{r_s}^{k_s}) \lambda_s \qquad [6.18]$$

$$\sum_{s \in \mathcal{R}/i \in s} \lambda_s = 1 \, ; \, \forall i \in P \qquad [6.19]$$

$$\lambda_s \in \{0, 1\} \, ; \, \forall s \in \mathcal{R} \qquad [6.20]$$

6.3.3.2. *Solution method and results*

We propose a column generation method to solve the relax version (RMP) of the master problem (MP). The problem of finding the column to insert is modeled by a linear model with mixed variables. Heuristics have been proposed to accelerate the search for columns with negative reduced cost. If the optimal solution of the RMP is not an integer, the integer version (IRMP) of this problem is resolved. In this case, it is not possible to know whether or not the solution obtained by the IRMP is optimal.

The proposed algorithm returns an actionable solution for all instances. It finds an optimal solution for 11% of instances. In 45% of instances, it makes it possible to find a lower limit that makes it possible to judge the quality of an integer solution found. An interesting observation was made on instances with "small" time windows, for which the algorithm found a lower limit in 86% of instances. For the instances in this configuration, the integer solution found is with a mean gap of 1.9%. Thus, we can state that in this configuration, the solutions returned are close to optimal. The computation time remains reasonable. These results form an initial version of the best-known solutions, which will be used in the future as the base for testing of future algorithms.

6.4. Conclusion

In this chapter, we presented a complex logistics problem in the hospital world. We proposed a hierarchization, with the aim of using scientific research carried out on the subproblems of this problem. Following this proposal, we established a procedure for solving the problem and the initial solutions proposed resulted in the implementation, within the Troyes hospital center, of a new organization of the journeys made by the vehicles with significant savings in terms of time and money, and with unexpected positive consequences such as a drop in the number of hours spent as waiting time by the drivers. In this procedure for the solution, we contributed significantly to the formalization and solution of problems that have not yet been taken up in the scientific milieu. This resulted in publications and, consequently, a scientific recognition of this work. Because of the partnership agreement between THC, the University of Technology of Troyes and the start-up Opta-Lp, the proposed solutions have been implemented in the form of a software package.

6.5. References

André V. (2011). Problème de livraison-collecte dans un environnement hospitalier: méthodes d'optimisation, modèle de simulation et couplages. PhD Thesis, Université Blaise Pascal, Clermont-Ferrand.

Belmecheri, F., Prins, C., Yalaoui, F., Amodeo, L. (2009). An ant colony optimization algorithm for a vehicle routing problem with heterogeneous fleet, mixed backhauls, and time windows. *IFAC Proceedings Volumes*, 42(4), 1550–1555.

Bent, R., Van Hentenryck, P. (2006). A two-stage hybrid algorithm for pickup and delivery vehicle routing problems with time windows. *Computers & Operations Research*, 33(4), 875–893.

Bettinelli, A., Ceselli, A., Righini, G. (2014). A branch-and-price algorithm for the multi-depot heterogeneous-fleet pickup and delivery problem with soft time windows. *Mathematical Programming Computation*, 6(2), 171–197.

Boldy, D.P. (1987). The relationship between decision support systems and operational research: health care examples. *European Journal of Operational Research*, 29(2), 128–134.

Boldy, D.P., O'Kane, P.C. (1982). Health operational research, a selective overview. *European Journal of Operational Research*, 10(1), 1–9.

Bourgeon, B., Constantin, A., Karolszyk, G., Marquot, J.-F., Pedrini, S., Landry, S., Diaz, A., Estampe, D. (2001). Évaluation des coûts logistiques hospitaliers en France et aux Pays-Bas. *Logistique & Management*, 9(1), 81–87.

Burke, E.K., De Causmaecker, P., Berghe, G.V., Van Landeghem, H. (2004). The state of the art of nurse rostering. *Journal of Scheduling*, 7(6), 441–499.

Cardoen, B., Demeulemeester, E., Beliën, J. (2010). Operating room planning and scheduling: a literature review. *European Journal of Operational Research*, 201(3), 921–932.

Castillo-Salazar, J.-A., Landa-Silva, D., Qu, R. (2016). Workforce scheduling and routing problems: literature survey and computational study. *Annals of Operations Research*, 239(1), 39–67.

Chow, G., Heaver, T.D., Henriksson, L.E. (1994). Logistics performance: definition and measurement. *International Journal of Physical Distribution & Logistics Management*, 24(1), 17–28.

Cordeau, J.-F. (2006). A branch-and-cut algorithm for the dial-a-ride problem. *Operations Research*, 54(3), 573–586.

Cordeau, J.-F., Laporte, G. (2003). A tabu search heuristic for the static multi-vehicle dial-a-ride problem. *Transportation Research Part B: Methodological*, 37(6), 579–594.

Cornuéjols, G. (2008). Valid inequalities for mixed integer linear programs. *Mathematical Programming*, 112(1), 3–44.

Dantzig, G.B., Wolfe, P. (1960). Decomposition principle for linear programs. *Operations Research*, 8(1), 101–111.

Davis, R.N. (2004). No more chances for supply-chain savings? Look again! Many hospitals assume they have exhausted opportunities to reduce supply-chain costs. but a well-coordinated, interdisciplinary effort may still yield substantial savings. *Healthcare Financial Management*, 58(1), 68–76.

Desrochers, M., Laporte, G. (1991). Improvements and extensions to the Miller-Tucker-Zemlin subtour elimination constraints. *Operations Research Letters*, 10(1), 27–36.

Dorigo, M., Gambardella, L.M. (1997). Ant colony system: a cooperative learning approach to the traveling salesman problem. *IEEE Transactions on Evolutionary Computation*, 1(1), 53–66.

Dumas, Y., Desrosiers, J., Soumis, F. (1991). The pickup and delivery problem with time windows. *European Journal of Operational Research*, 54(1), 7–22.

Fries, B.E. (1976). Bibliography of operations research in health-care systems. *Operations Research*, 24(5), 801–814.

Glover, F. (1989). Tabu search—part I. *ORSA Journal on Computing*, 1(3), 190–206.

Goss, S., Aron, S., Deneubourg, J.-L., Pasteels, J.-M. (1989). Self-organized shortcuts in the argentine ant. *Naturwissenschaften*, 76(12), 579–581.

Grandinetti, L., Guerriero, F., Pezzella, F., Pisacane, O. (2014). The multi-objective multi-vehicle pickup and delivery problem with time windows. *Procedia – Social and Behavioral Sciences*, 111, 203–212.

Henning, W.K. (1980). The financial impact of materials management. *Hospital Financial Management*, 34(2), 36–42.

Irnich, S. (2000). A multi-depot pickup and delivery problem with a single hub and heterogeneous vehicles. *European Journal of Operational Research*, 122(2), 310–328.

Kergosien, Y., Lenté, C., Piton, D., Billaut, J.C. (2011). A tabu search heuristic for a dynamic transportation problem of patients between care units. *HAL*, hal-00488270.

Kergosien, Y., Lenté, C., Billaut, J-C., Perrin, S. (2013). Metaheuristic algorithms for solving two interconnected vehicle routing problems in a hospital complex. *Computers & Operations Research*, 40(10), 2508–2518.

Kowalski, J.C. (1991). Materials management crucial to overall efficiency. *Healthcare Financial Management: Journal of the Healthcare Financial Management Association*, 45(1), 40–42.

Li, H., Lim, A. (2003). A metaheuristic for the pickup and delivery problem with time windows. *International Journal on Artificial Intelligence Tools*, 12(02), 173–186.

Li, L.X., Benton, W.C. (1996). Performance measurement criteria in health care organizations: review and future research directions. *European Journal of Operational Research*, 93(3), 449–468.

Liberatore, M.J., Nydick, R.L. (2008). The analytic hierarchy process in medical and health care decision making: A literature review. *European Journal of Operational Research*, 189(1), 194–207.

Liu, F.-H., Shen, S.-Y. (1999). The fleet size and mix vehicle routing problem with time windows. *Journal of the Operational Research Society*, 50(7), 721–732.

Medaglia, A.L., Villegas, J.-G., Rodríguez-Coca, D.-M. (2009). Hybrid bi-objective evolutionary algorithms for the design of a hospital waste management network. *Journal of Heuristics*, 15(2), 153.

Mitchell, M., Crutchfield, J.P., Das, R. (1996). Evolving cellular automata with genetic algorithms: a review of recent work. *Proceedings of the First International Conference on Evolutionary Computation and Its Applications (EvCA'96)*. Russian Academy of Sciences, Moscow.

Nagata, Y., Kobayashi, S. (2010). *Guided Ejection Search for the Pickup and Delivery Problem with Time Windows*. Springer, Berlin.

Nalepa, J., Blocho, M. (2016). Enhanced guided ejection search for the pickup and delivery problem with time windows. *Lecture Notes in Computer Science*, 9621, 388–398.

Noumbissi Tchoupo, M.N., Yalaoui, A., Amodeo, L., Yaloui, F., Lutz, F. (2016). Problème de collectes et livraisons avec fenêtres de temps et flotte homogène. University assignment, Université de Technologie de Troyes, Troyes.

Noumbissi Tchoupo, M.N., Yalaoui, A., Amodeo, L., Yalaoui, F., Lutz, F. (2017). Ant colony optimization algorithm for pickup and delivery problem with time windows. In *Methodologies and Applications Optimization and Decision Science*, Sforza, A., Sterle, C. (eds), Springer, Berlin, 181–191.

Qu, Y., Bard, J.F. (2013). The heterogeneous pickup and delivery problem with configurable vehicle capacity. *Transportation Research Part C: Emerging Technologies*, 32, 1–20.

Ropke, S., Pisinger, D. (2006). An adaptive large neighborhood search heuristic for the pickup and delivery problem with time windows. *Transportation Science*, 40(4), 455–472.

Rosenhead, J. (1978). Operational research in health services planning. *European Journal of Operational Research*, 2(2), 75–85.

Shih, L.-H., Chang, H.-C. (2001). A routing and scheduling system for infectious waste pickup. *Environmental Modeling & Assessment*, 6(4), 261–269.

Swaminathan, J.M. (2003). Decision support for allocating scarce drugs. *Interfaces*, 33(2), 1–11.

Volland, J., Fügener, A., Schoenfelder, J., Brunner, J.O. (2017). Material logistics in hospitals: a literature review. *Omega*, 69, 82–101.

Wiers, V.C.S. (1997). A review of the applicability of OR and AI scheduling techniques in practice. *Omega*, 25(2), 145–153.

Xu, H., Chen, Z.-L., Rajagopal, S., Arunapuram, S. (2003). Solving a practical pickup and delivery problem. *Transportation Science*, 37(3), 347–364.

List of Authors

Mohamed AFILAL
Capgemini
Paris
France

Lionel AMODEO
University of Technology of Troyes
France

Philippe BLUA
Champagne Sud hospitals
Troyes
France

Michaël DE BLOCK
Centre hospitalier régional
de Metz-Thionville
France

Frédéric DUGARDIN
University of Technology of Troyes
France

David LAPLANCHE
Champagne Sud hospitals
Troyes
France

Frédéric LUTZ
Centre hospitalier Geneviève
De Gaulle Anthonioz de Saint-Dizier
Centre hospitalier de Vitry-le-François
EHPAD de Thiéblemont-Farémont
France

Moïse NOUMBISSI TCHOUPO
Champagne Sud hospitals
Troyes
France

Stéphane SANCHEZ
Champagne Sud hospitals
Troyes
France

Alice YALAOUI
University of Technology of Troyes
France

Farouk YALAOUI
University of Technology of Troyes
France

Index

Other titles from

in

Systems and Industrial Engineering – Robotics

2019

ANDRÉ Jean-Claude
Industry 4.0: Paradoxes and Conflicts

BENSALAH Mounir, ELOUADI Abdelmajid, MHARZI Hassan
Railway Information Modeling RIM: The Track to Rail Modernization

BRIFFAUT Jean-Pierre
From Complexity in the Natural Sciences to Complexity in Operations Management Systems
(Systems of Systems Complexity Set – Volume 1)

BUDINGER Marc, HAZYUK Ion, COÏC Clément
Multi-Physics Modeling of Technological Systems

FLAUS Jean-Marie
Cybersecurity of Industrial Systems

KUMAR Kaushik, DAVIM Paulo J.
Optimization for Engineering Problems

TRIGEASSOU Jean-Claude, MAAMRI Nezha
Analysis, Modeling and Stability of Fractional Order Differential Systems 1

VANDERHAEGEN Frédéric, MAAOUI Choubeila, SALLAK Mohamed,
BERDJAG Denis
Automation Challenges of Socio-technical Systems

2018

BERRAH Lamia, CLIVILLÉ Vincent, FOULLOY Laurent
*Industrial Objectives and Industrial Performance: Concepts and Fuzzy
Handling*

GONZALEZ-FELIU Jesus
Sustainable Urban Logistics: Planning and Evaluation

GROUS Ammar
Applied Mechanical Design

LEROY Alain
Production Availability and Reliability: Use in the Oil and Gas Industry

MARÉ Jean-Charles
*Aerospace Actuators 3: European Commercial Aircraft and
Tiltrotor Aircraft*

MAXA Jean-Aimé, BEN MAHMOUD Mohamed Slim, LARRIEU Nicolas
*Model-driven Development for Embedded Software: Application to
Communications for Drone Swarm*

MBIHI Jean
*Analog Automation and Digital Feedback Control Techniques
Advanced Techniques and Technology of Computer-Aided Feedback Control*

MORANA Joëlle
Logistics

SIMON Christophe, WEBER Philippe, SALLAK Mohamed
*Data Uncertainty and Important Measures
(Systems Dependability Assessment Set – Volume 3)*

TANIGUCHI Eiichi, THOMPSON Russell G.
City Logistics 1: New Opportunities and Challenges
City Logistics 2: Modeling and Planning Initiatives
City Logistics 3: Towards Sustainable and Liveable Cities

ZELM Martin, JAEKEL Frank-Walter, DOUMEINGTS Guy, WOLLSCHLAEGER Martin
Enterprise Interoperability: Smart Services and Business Impact of Enterprise Interoperability

2017

ANDRÉ Jean-Claude
From Additive Manufacturing to 3D/4D Printing 1: From Concepts to Achievements
From Additive Manufacturing to 3D/4D Printing 2: Current Techniques, Improvements and their Limitations
From Additive Manufacturing to 3D/4D Printing 3: Breakthrough Innovations: Programmable Material, 4D Printing and Bio-printing

ARCHIMÈDE Bernard, VALLESPIR Bruno
Enterprise Interoperability: INTEROP-PGSO Vision

CAMMAN Christelle, FIORE Claude, LIVOLSI Laurent, QUERRO Pascal
Supply Chain Management and Business Performance: The VASC Model

FEYEL Philippe
Robust Control, Optimization with Metaheuristics

MARÉ Jean-Charles
Aerospace Actuators 2: Signal-by-Wire and Power-by-Wire

POPESCU Dumitru, AMIRA Gharbi, STEFANOIU Dan, BORNE Pierre
Process Control Design for Industrial Applications

RÉVEILLAC Jean-Michel
Modeling and Simulation of Logistics Flows 1: Theory and Fundamentals
Modeling and Simulation of Logistics Flows 2: Dashboards, Traffic Planning and Management
Modeling and Simulation of Logistics Flows 3: Discrete and Continuous Flows in 2D/3D

2016

ANDRÉ Michel, SAMARAS Zissis
Energy and Environment
(Research for Innovative Transports Set - Volume 1)

AUBRY Jean-François, BRINZEI Nicolae, MAZOUNI Mohammed-Habib
Systems Dependability Assessment: Benefits of Petri Net Models (Systems Dependability Assessment Set - Volume 1)

BLANQUART Corinne, CLAUSEN Uwe, JACOB Bernard
Towards Innovative Freight and Logistics (Research for Innovative Transports Set - Volume 2)

COHEN Simon, YANNIS George
Traffic Management (Research for Innovative Transports Set - Volume 3)

MARÉ Jean-Charles
Aerospace Actuators 1: Needs, Reliability and Hydraulic Power Solutions

REZG Nidhal, HAJEJ Zied, BOSCHIAN-CAMPANER Valerio
Production and Maintenance Optimization Problems: Logistic Constraints and Leasing Warranty Services

TORRENTI Jean-Michel, LA TORRE Francesca
Materials and Infrastructures 1 (Research for Innovative Transports Set - Volume 5A)
Materials and Infrastructures 2 (Research for Innovative Transports Set - Volume 5B)

WEBER Philippe, SIMON Christophe
Benefits of Bayesian Network Models
(Systems Dependability Assessment Set – Volume 2)

NI Zhenjiang, PACORET Céline, BENOSMAN Ryad, RÉGNIER Stéphane
Haptic Feedback Teleoperation of Optical Tweezers

OUSTALOUP Alain
Diversity and Non-integer Differentiation for System Dynamics

REZG Nidhal, DELLAGI Sofien, KHATAD Abdelhakim
Joint Optimization of Maintenance and Production Policies

STEFANOIU Dan, BORNE Pierre, POPESCU Dumitru, FILIP Florin Gh.,
EL KAMEL Abdelkader
*Optimization in Engineering Sciences: Metaheuristics, Stochastic Methods
and Decision Support*

2013

ALAZARD Daniel
Reverse Engineering in Control Design

ARIOUI Hichem, NEHAOUA Lamri
Driving Simulation

CHADLI Mohammed, COPPIER Hervé
Command-control for Real-time Systems

DAAFOUZ Jamal, TARBOURIECH Sophie, SIGALOTTI Mario
Hybrid Systems with Constraints

FEYEL Philippe
Loop-shaping Robust Control

FLAUS Jean-Marie
Risk Analysis: Socio-technical and Industrial Systems

FRIBOURG Laurent, SOULAT Romain
*Control of Switching Systems by Invariance Analysis: Application to Power
Electronics*

GROSSARD Mathieu, REGNIER Stéphane, CHAILLET Nicolas
Flexible Robotics: Applications to Multiscale Manipulations

GRUNN Emmanuel, PHAM Anh Tuan
Modeling of Complex Systems: Application to Aeronautical Dynamics

HABIB Maki K., DAVIM J. Paulo
Interdisciplinary Mechatronics: Engineering Science and Research Development

HAMMADI Slim, KSOURI Mekki
Multimodal Transport Systems

JARBOUI Bassem, SIARRY Patrick, TEGHEM Jacques
Metaheuristics for Production Scheduling

KIRILLOV Oleg N., PELINOVSKY Dmitry E.
Nonlinear Physical Systems

LE Vu Tuan Hieu, STOICA Cristina, ALAMO Teodoro, CAMACHO Eduardo F., DUMUR Didier
Zonotopes: From Guaranteed State-estimation to Control

MACHADO Carolina, DAVIM J. Paulo
Management and Engineering Innovation

MORANA Joëlle
Sustainable Supply Chain Management

SANDOU Guillaume
Metaheuristic Optimization for the Design of Automatic Control Laws

STOICAN Florin, OLARU Sorin
Set-theoretic Fault Detection in Multisensor Systems

2012

AÏT-KADI Daoud, CHOUINARD Marc, MARCOTTE Suzanne, RIOPEL Diane
Sustainable Reverse Logistics Network: Engineering and Management

BORNE Pierre, POPESCU Dumitru, FILIP Florin G., STEFANOIU Dan
Optimization in Engineering Sciences: Exact Methods

CHADLI Mohammed, BORNE Pierre
Multiple Models Approach in Automation: Takagi-Sugeno Fuzzy Systems

DAVIM J. Paulo
Lasers in Manufacturing

DECLERCK Philippe
Discrete Event Systems in Dioid Algebra and Conventional Algebra

DOUMIATI Moustapha, CHARARA Ali, VICTORINO Alessandro, LECHNER Daniel
Vehicle Dynamics Estimation using Kalman Filtering: Experimental Validation

GUERRERO José A, LOZANO Rogelio
Flight Formation Control

HAMMADI Slim, KSOURI Mekki
Advanced Mobility and Transport Engineering

MAILLARD Pierre
Competitive Quality Strategies

MATTA Nada, VANDENBOOMGAERDE Yves, ARLAT Jean
Supervision and Safety of Complex Systems

POLER Raul *et al.*
Intelligent Non-hierarchical Manufacturing Networks

TROCCAZ Jocelyne
Medical Robotics

YALAOUI Alice, CHEHADE Hicham, YALAOUI Farouk, AMODEO Lionel
Optimization of Logistics

ZELM Martin *et al.*
Enterprise Interoperability –I-EASA12 Proceedings

2011

CANTOT Pascal, LUZEAUX Dominique
Simulation and Modeling of Systems of Systems

DAVIM J. Paulo
Mechatronics

DAVIM J. Paulo
Wood Machining

GROUS Ammar
Applied Metrology for Manufacturing Engineering

KOLSKI Christophe
Human–Computer Interactions in Transport

LUZEAUX Dominique, RUAULT Jean-René, WIPPLER Jean-Luc
Complex Systems and Systems of Systems Engineering

ZELM Martin, *et al.*
Enterprise Interoperability: IWEI2011 Proceedings

2010

BOTTA-GENOULAZ Valérie, CAMPAGNE Jean-Pierre, LLERENA Daniel, PELLEGRIN Claude
Supply Chain Performance / Collaboration, Alignement and Coordination

BOURLÈS Henri, GODFREY K.C. Kwan
Linear Systems

BOURRIÈRES Jean-Paul
Proceedings of CEISIE'09

CHAILLET Nicolas, REGNIER Stéphane
Microrobotics for Micromanipulation

DAVIM J. Paulo
Sustainable Manufacturing

GIORDANO Max, MATHIEU Luc, VILLENEUVE François
Product Life-Cycle Management / Geometric Variations

LOZANO Rogelio
Unmanned Aerial Vehicles / Embedded Control

LUZEAUX Dominique, RUAULT Jean-René
Systems of Systems

VILLENEUVE François, MATHIEU Luc
Geometric Tolerancing of Products

2009

DIAZ Michel
Petri Nets / Fundamental Models, Verification and Applications

OZEL Tugrul, DAVIM J. Paulo
Intelligent Machining

PITRAT Jacques
Artificial Beings

2008

ARTIGUES Christian, DEMASSEY Sophie, NERON Emmanuel
Resources–Constrained Project Scheduling

BILLAUT Jean-Charles, MOUKRIM Aziz, SANLAVILLE Eric
Flexibility and Robustness in Scheduling

DOCHAIN Denis
Bioprocess Control

LOPEZ Pierre, ROUBELLAT François
Production Scheduling

THIERRY Caroline, THOMAS André, BEL Gérard
Supply Chain Simulation and Management

2007

DE LARMINAT Philippe
Analysis and Control of Linear Systems

DOMBRE Etienne, KHALIL Wisama
Robot Manipulators

LAMNABHI Françoise *et al.*
Taming Heterogeneity and Complexity of Embedded Control

Printed and bound by CPI Group (UK) Ltd, Croydon, CR0 4YY